Globalization and Militarism

GLOBALIZATION

Series Editors
Manfred B. Steger
*Illinois State University, University of Hawai'i—Manoa,
and Royal Melbourne Institute of Technology*
and
Terrell Carver
University of Bristol

"Globalization" has become *the* buzzword of our time. But what does it mean? Rather than forcing a complicated social phenomenon into a single analytical framework, this series seeks to present globalization as a multidimensional process constituted by complex, often contradictory interactions of global, regional, and local aspects of social life. Since conventional disciplinary borders and lines of demarcation are losing their old rationales in a globalizing world, authors in this series apply an interdisciplinary framework to the study of globalization. In short, the main purpose and objective of this series is to support subject-specific inquiries into the dynamics and effects of contemporary globalization and its varying impacts across, between, and within societies.

Globalization and War
Tarak Barkawi

Globalization and American Popular Culture
Lane Crothers

Globalization and Militarism
Cynthia Enloe

Globalization and Law
Adam Gearey

Globalization and Feminist Activism
Mary E. Hawkesworth

Globalization and Terrorism
Jamal R. Nassar

Globalization and Culture
Jan Nederveen Pieterse

Globalization and International Political Economy
Mark Rupert and M. Scott Solomon

Globalism
Manfred B. Steger

Rethinking Globalism
Edited by Manfred B. Steger

Globaloney
Michael Veseth

 Supported by the Globalization Research Center at the University of Hawai'i, Manoa

GLOBALIZATION AND MILITARISM

Feminists Make the Link

CYNTHIA ENLOE

ROWMAN & LITTLEFIELD PUBLISHERS, INC.
Lanham • Boulder • New York • Toronto • Plymouth, UK

ROWMAN & LITTLEFIELD PUBLISHERS, INC.

Published in the United States of America
by Rowman & Littlefield Publishers, Inc.
A wholly owned subsidiary of The Rowman & Littlefield Publishing Group, Inc.
4501 Forbes Boulevard, Suite 200, Lanham, Maryland 20706
www.rowmanlittlefield.com

Estover Road, Plymouth PL6 7PY, United Kingdom

Some material in chapters 2, 3, 4, and 7 was originally translated into Japanese
by Kozue Akibayashi, edited by the Ochanomizu University Institute for
Gender Studies, and published by Ochanomizu Shobo, Publishers, under the
title *Exploring Militarism and International Politics with a Feminist Curiosity*
(2004), by Cynthia Enloe.

British Library Cataloguing in Publication Information Available

Library of Congress Cataloging-in-Publication Data
Enloe, Cynthia H., 1938–
    Globalization and militarism : feminists make the link / Cynthia Enloe.
       p.   cm.—(Globalization)
    Includes bibliographical references and index.
    ISBN-13: 978-0-7425-4111-5 (cloth : alk. paper)
    ISBN-10: 0-7425-4111-8 (cloth : alk. paper)
    ISBN-13: 978-0-7425-4112-2 (pbk. : alk. paper)
    ISBN-10: 0-7425-4112-6 (pbk. : alk. paper)
    1. Globalization.   2. Militarism.   3. Women and the military.
    4. Women soldiers.   5. Disarmament.   I. Title.
JZ1318.E65   2007
303.48'2—dc22
                                                          2006033653

Printed in the United States of America

♾ ™ The paper used in this publication meets the minimum requirements of
American National Standard for Information Sciences—Permanence of Paper
for Printed Library Materials, ANSI/NISO Z39.48-1992.

This book is dedicated to
Ann, Spike, Sandy, Marysia, Anne, Jindy,
Gillian, Kathy, Jane, Marianne, Judith, Kathy, Francine, Shirin, Lily,
Terrell, Jill, Carol, Catherine, Deborah, Judith, Rekha, Meredith, Simona,
Christine, and all the smart, energetic feminist scholars who have
transformed International Relations

CONTENTS

PREFACE

This book had its first incarnation as a series of lectures given in Tokyo on the eve of the March 2003 U.S.-led invasion of Iraq. Many Japanese were intently following the UN debates and the military buildup. The Japanese usually keep a close eye on the United States—its styles, its movies, its economy, its politics, its sports (while I was there, Ichiro Suzuki's performance in spring training with the Seattle Mariners was the topic of daily coverage, and Michael Moore's film *Bowling for Columbine* was drawing large audiences in movie theaters around the country). But in the early months of 2003, many Japanese were worried that Washington would pressure Japanese officials to make at least a token gesture of military involvement in the United States' invasion of Iraq—despite the Japanese constitution, which forbids any Japanese military involvement in aggressive operations.

The talks I gave in Tokyo were organized by the Institute for Gender Studies at Ochanomizu University, one of Japan's premier centers for women's studies teaching and research. The eighty or so people who came to each talk held at this famous national women's university were drawn by a desire to make sense of complex international politics combined with an interest in exploring the ways that feminist analysis might shed light on international politics.

I learned a great deal from preparing those talks (e.g., trying to make sure that I didn't fall into any U.S.-centric assumptions) and especially, from taking part in the lively discussions that followed each talk, first in the large auditorium and then over red wine and sandwiches at the Institute for Gender Studies' crowded offices across campus. It was a wonderful three months.

The book you are about to read grows out of those talks and the book subsequently published in Japanese, in which I tried to capture the spirit of feminist international political inquiry that was at the heart of the lecture series. But the present book is necessarily different. I have tried to hold on to that original non-U.S.-centric perspective, but I also have done a lot of revising and updating.

This current book thus has been affected by five years of war in Afghanistan, three years of war in Iraq, and years of local and international efforts to end wars in the former Yugoslavia, Israel, Lebanon, Palestine, Chechnya, Congo, Liberia, Sierra Leone, Sudan, East Timor, Nepal, and Sri Lanka. Only some of those efforts—attempts to globalize *de*militarization—have proved successful.

Over the last three years feminist explorations into globalization and militarization have been burgeoning. I am in debt to all the researchers and activists who have done this important work. They come from many countries. It is impossible to get a realistic grip on militarizing processes and globalizing processes if one listens to or reads only observers coming from a handful of countries. So as you read the chapters ahead, imagine me listening to Canadian feminists discussing the still-masculinized politics of their own country's much-praised UN peacekeeping operations, picture me sitting at a café poring over the latest reports published by the Belgrade Women in Black peace activists, think of me reading and then rereading letters, clippings, and e-mails from researchers and activist friends in Tel Aviv, Istanbul, Santiago, Boston, Philadelphia, Tokyo, Oslo, Stockholm, Geneva, Toronto, Dublin, Brighton, Johannesburg, and Seoul. I have sought to do justice to all of their insights here.

My special thanks for their doing so much to shape the thinking that informs this book go to all the members of the wonderful Feminist Theory and Gender Section of the International Studies Association, to whom this book is dedicated, as well as to Ayse Gul Altinay, Rela Mezali, Orna Sasson-Levy, Gila Svirsky, Ariane Brunet, Lepa Mladjenovic, Stasa Zajovic, Ximena Bunster, Ailbhe Smyth, Rita Arditti, Cynthia Cockburn, Carol Cohn, Saralee Hamilton, Insook Kwon, Felicity Hill, Nadine Puechguirbal, Aaron Belkin, Ann

Smith, Vanessa Farr, Dyan Mazurana, Lory Manning, Wenona Giles, Sandra Whitworth, Catherine Lutz, Kathy Ferguson, Keith Severin, and Bob Benewick. They each, and all together, remind me of what it means to stay intellectually curious and politically engaged, even in such a militarized world.

I am fortunate indeed to be partners with Joni Seager, worldly feminist geographer and environmentalist, for whom no place is too remote and no authority immune to challenge.

The Japanese feminist researchers of Ochanomizu University's Institute for Gender Studies who planted the seeds for the Tokyo lecture series and then oversaw the publication of the resultant Japanese book deserve special thanks: Professors Kaoru Tachi and Ruri Ito and all the splendid feminists on the staffs of the institute and its publishing house.

The thoughtfully provocative scholars who launched this new Rowman & Littlefield innovative book series on globalization politics are Professors Terrell Carver and Manfred Steger. It was Terrell Carver, himself a major interrogator of masculinity, who convinced me that one book in the series should tackle the interplay of militarization and globalization *and* that an explicitly feminist approach would be appealing to faculty members and their students in courses on international and global affairs. I am indebted to them both.

At Rowman & Littlefield, Jennifer Knerr was the editor who first saw the promise in this ambitious globalization publishing project. When she moved on to other exciting publishing ventures, the editor's baton was energetically picked up by Susan McEachern. Every book you read has been made more readable because of the professional attention devoted to it by an editor.

As they say, "It takes a village." For this book to reach your hands, it has taken a globalized feminist village.

CRAFTING A GLOBAL "FEMINIST CURIOSITY" TO MAKE SENSE OF GLOBALIZED MILITARISM: TALLYING IMPACTS, EXPOSING CAUSES

Developing a "curiosity" involves exploring, questioning—refusing to take something for granted. One is *not* curious about the things one takes for granted. For instance, most of us most of the time (unless we have a rotten cold or have started going to yoga classes) aren't very curious about breathing. Most of us most of the time (unless we read the science pages of our newspapers) also don't spend much time wondering about the melting arctic ice caps.

A major theme we will chart here is "feminist curiosity": How to develop it? What's distinctive about it? We will discover what it is that a feminist curiosity can reveal about the workings of globalization and militarization—and track the links *between* them—that we would otherwise miss. In other words, this is a very practical, down-to-earth enterprise.

Developing a new kind of curiosity is not just academic. It takes energy. It is political. It is cultural. It is personal. To insist upon posing questions about things that other people take for granted can be a political act.

A feminist curiosity is a crucial tool to use today in making sense of the links between two of the world's most potent trends: *globalization* and *militarization*.

Like any "ization" (e.g., industrialization, urbanization), globalization and militarization are actually many-layered processes of transformation. For instance, it turns out to be possible to track, step by step, strategic decision by strategic decision, precisely how the Nazi regime of 1930s Germany transformed the conscience of so many ordinary Germans. Advertising techniques and popular moviemaking played central roles (Koonz 2003). Thus you will need to watch each over time—a quick snapshot isn't going to reveal much—and you'll need to keep your eye on several layers at once, watching individuals change and at the same time paying attention to changes occurring in local communities, public institutions, companies, and whole societies. It's a tall order. Using a feminist curiosity should help you do it more realistically and with more reliable results.

Globalization is the step-by-step process by which anything—a movie industry, vegetable production, law enforcement, banking, the nursing profession, higher education, an individual's own sense of identity, human rights, environmental activism, or a women's movement—becomes more interdependent and coordinated across national borders. The rubber industry, for instance, has been globalized almost from its very start.

Rubber. The first time I wondered where the rubber for my car's tires came from was when I was a graduate student living for a year in Malaysia trying to understand the ethnic tensions inside this former British colony's complex education system. My little apartment, though, was in a new development just outside the capital on land carved out of a rubber plantation. So in addition to education politics, I began to ponder rubber. There were rubber trees just outside my back door. In the early morning I watched rubber tappers working, skillfully slicing crescent-shaped cuts into the dappled bark of the slender rubber trees, then placing underneath the new cuts small cups into which the rubber tree's treasure, white liquid latex, would drip. Standing there in the early morning tropical light, I thought about the tires on my VW Beetle. But I don't think I realized that I was watching globalization at work.

For it was British scientists a century ago who surreptitiously took rubber trees from Brazil to their famous Kew botanical gardens in England, developed a commercial strain of rubber trees, transplanted them in their then British-ruled colony of Malaya in Southeast Asia, and hired thousands of Indian migrant workers to tap the white fluid latex flowing from the slim rubber trees on their vast plantations. The result: Dunlop, a British company operating rubber plantations in Malaya, became an international powerhouse when the development of the auto industry made rubber tires essential to modern transportation worldwide. The American company Firestone similarly used Liberia and France's Michelin used Vietnam to develop their global tire and rubber businesses. And other iconic American companies such as Singer, maker of the famous Singer sewing machines, were consciously developing global marketing strategies by the early twentieth century (Domosh 2006). So globalizing trends—in science, political control, labor migration, product marketing—are not new. What is new is the scale and breadth of globalizing trends since the late twentieth century.

Often *globalization* is used as a shorthand label only for the worldwide sprawl of capitalist business organizations and flows of technology, labor, and capital designed to enhance the profits of those businesses. Likewise, then, *antiglobalization* is used to refer to the many-stranded social movement inspired by critiques of that capitalist globalizing trend. But it is more useful to understand that globalization can happen to anything, not just to profit-seeking companies and their products and employees. In fact, the antiglobalization movement, with its loose but often effective networks of environmental activists, antisweatshop activists, prodemocracy advocates, and local culture defenders, is itself a major result of globalizing trends: activists in Nigeria are now trading information and strategic lessons with people in Canada and India.

On the other hand, it is true that not everyone enters into globalization with equal resources: not everyone can afford jet travel; not everyone has easy access to the Internet; not everyone has scientific laboratories or banking credit at their fingertips; not everyone has equal access to English, the increasingly dominant "lingua franca" of globalized communication; not everyone gets to discuss their international issues privately over cocktails with a senator.

Militarization may be a less familiar concept. But it too is a trans-

3

forming process that happens over time—sometimes rapidly, though often at a slow, hard-to-spot creep. And like the process of globalization, militarizing trends can simultaneously change the influence one person has on another, can alter how stories are interpreted, can turn meanings upside down. To become militarized is to adopt militaristic values (e.g., a belief in hierarchy, obedience, and the use of force) and priorities as one's own, to see military solutions as particularly effective, to see the world as a dangerous place best approached with militaristic attitudes. These changes may take generations to occur, or they may happen suddenly as the response to a particular trauma. Most of the people in the world who are militarized are not themselves in uniform. Most militarized people are civilians.

A husband and wife's marriage can become militarized if the husband decides to enlist in his country's military and that military operates on the assumption that a soldier's spouse will put the needs of the soldier in the family ahead of any other marital need. If a wife finishes her engineering degree and decides to accept a job offer to work for a large corporation that relies on defense contracts from governments and expects its engineers to accept a culture of secrecy, that can create deep pockets of silence within the couple's home life. Similarly, a town's elected officials can become militarized if they begin to think that getting and keeping a nearby military base enhances the town's economic health or if they believe a local weapons-producing corporation offers the best chance for sustaining decently paid jobs for their residents.

A government's international intelligence service can be militarized if intelligence gathering is done chiefly by the country's department of defense. Even if an independent intelligence agency exists on the government's organizational chart, intelligence gathering and, especially important, the interpreting of that intelligence, can become militarized if in daily reality it is the defense bureaucracy that possesses the greater budget and resources to conduct its own intelligence operations—and the country's elected representatives accept this as normal or even effective.

A country's international borders likewise can become militarized if a majority of voters and their representatives begin to think that danger lurks on the other side of those borders, dangers that must be addressed not through cultural understanding, diplomatic negotiations, immigration regulations, and ordinary policing, but instead through fortification, militarized policing, and even the deployment of soldiers. Such border transformations can spark intense public discussions and debates over whether militarization is the most useful process by which to address the movement of peoples from state to state in today's increasingly globalized world.

A civilian court judge can become militarized if that judge begins to believe that she or he must defer to a government lawyer's claims that, when a government agency is sued by a civilian plaintiff, the government's need to protect "national security" trumps all other claims before the court. Judicial deference in the face of executive branch claims of national security necessity is one of the most common modes of judges' militarization. That is, militarization can look less like conventional aggressiveness and more like deferential passivity.

Ordinary citizens can become militarized whenever they start to think that the world is so dangerous that the necessarily slow processes of legislative hearings, compromise, and open voting don't match the sense of speed and urgency—and maybe secrecy—they have come to think are needed to address those alleged dangers. This is the point at which officials in the executive wing of government—presidents, prime ministers, politically appointed officials, career civil servants—may think they have been given the green light to act behind the legislature's back, without public oversight, in the name of protecting the public from the perceived danger. If some members of the elected legislature also share this sense of danger and urgency and the resultant impatience with compromise and transparency, then that green light will shine all the more brightly. An elected legislator becomes militarized when she or he starts to demote civil liberties to second place behind purported military necessity. Any civilian voter assessing the legislators becomes militarized when she or he begins to see military solutions to international problems as more effective than the often painfully slow and complex diplomatic solutions.

A globalizing corporation becomes militarized insofar as its executives come to believe that its overseas factories will be more secure if the foreign government is willing to use military troops or militarized police to put down labor protests.

This book explores how these two potent contemporary trends—globalization and militarization—often feed each other. That is, as the example of the corporation that locates its factories in a country whose government is quick to wield military force against employees who demonstrate for better working conditions shows, *globalization can become militarized.* Globalization depends on militarization whenever militarized ideas about national security come to be seen as central to creating or sustaining certain international relationships.

Similarly, *militarization can be globalized.* Think of all the national and international sales of rifles, land mines, armored vehicles, submarines, fighter aircraft, radar systems, guided missiles, and unmanned surveillance aircraft. There are so many players—scientists, engineers, producers, sellers, middlemen, buyers, and users—involved that peace advocates have formed several independent, globally conscious groups (e.g., the Small Arms Survey, based in Geneva, Switzerland, and the Swedish Institute for Peace Research in Stockholm) just to track the complex flows of large and small arms, together worth billions of dollars.

For instance, just looking at the contracts won by the largest military defense corporations from the U.S. Department of Defense in fiscal year 2005, we see that Lockheed Martin tops the list with $19.45 billion worth (that amounts to 7.2 percent of the total Pentagon business), followed closely by Boeing with $18.32 billion. Third and fourth among the American defense manufacturing giants are Northrop Grumman and General Dynamics, respectively. Moving down the list, there is Raytheon in fifth place and Halliburton in sixth. Each of these corporations shapes the lives of thousands of employees—and the family members and local communities that depend on their wages. Number seven on the list caught some observers' eyes: It was not American. The British company BAE Systems was the only non-U.S. company in the "top ten" for 2005. It had benefited from the "special relationship" between the U.S. and British governments in foreign policy, which persuaded Pentagon officials that, while not American, BAE could be trusted with contracts for sensitive weaponry. BAE's executives said it was not really an anomaly but an indicator of more to come—namely, defense manufacturers headquartered in diverse countries seeking profitable weapons contracts from any government eager to buy (Wayne 2006).

While it is usually the large companies producing the large weapons systems that make the news, small weapons kill more people day in and day out around the world. Where do the guns and ammunition that are causing death and dislocation among thousands of civilians in the Darfur region of Sudan come from? How do they get from their manufacturers to Sudan? Who is profiting?

Consider the recent emergence of globally active private military contractors such as Blackwater USA. Unlike the more familiar defense manufacturers, private military contractors actually provide, for a substantial fee, the services formerly provided by government militaries and police forces—guarding embassies and mines, providing food for soldiers, running supply convoys. By 2006, in Iraq alone, nearly 50,000 private military and security personnel had been contracted by the U.S. government, private businesses (including newspapers and television companies), and the fledgling Iraqi government to provide various services (Koppel 2006; Holmquist 2005). In addition, there are scores of companies—some little known to the public, others as well known as Halliburton, AT&T, Pizza Hut, and Burger King—that may not deliver armed men overseas, but do make profits by providing goods and services to soldiers in war zones, including Iraq.

Or imagine a map of the world showing all the military bases— large and small—that just the U.S. government operates. Today, there are American military bases from Cuba to San Diego to Britain and Italy, from Qatar to North Carolina to Japan, from Bulgaria and Bosnia to Kazakhstan, Aruba, and Guam. Now, thirty years after the end of the brutal Vietnam-United States War, there are even negotiations going on between the U.S. and Vietnamese governments to allow the U.S. Navy to use Vietnam's port Da Nang. Every one of these American bases is the result of bargaining and pressure and formal agreements between the U.S. government and the officials of another country or territory. These bases and their immediate neighborhoods take the mundane forms of fences, tarmac, playgrounds, bowling alleys, bars, discos, grocery stores, clinics, tattoo parlors, tailors, mechanics shops, target ranges, file cabinets, memos, e-mails, love letters, sexually transmitted diseases, takeoffs, landings, parades, and pornographic pin-ups. Together, however, these everyday base fixtures and operations and the negotiations that create and sustain them add up to a globalization of militarization.

Again, some of these globalizing militarization engines were fired up more than a century ago. The imperial governments of Britain, France, the Netherlands, Spain, Portugal, the United States, and Belgium deliberately exported their own models of militaries to the countries they colonized around the world. Britain sought to replicate the British army in India, Nigeria, Malaysia, Fiji, Australia, and Egypt, complete with its own homegrown presumptions about ethnic hierarchies and notions of "martial races"—that is, ethnic groups whose men were imagined by the colonizers to be "traditional warriors" (Barkawi 2006). Britain's imperial rivals did the same in Indonesia, Vietnam, Mozambique, the Philippines, Senegal, Algeria, Peru, and Mexico (Enloe 1980). Still today, the British military is seeking recruits into its own military from young men in its former colonies, especially Fiji and Nepal (for its famed Gurkha regiments) (Gillan 2005). When you next hear about Gurkhas serving in the British peacekeeping forces in Bosnia or Kosovo, think of the long-lasting gendered militarized legacies of imperialism, as well as the hopes of young men and their parents in impoverished former colonies.

So the globalization of militarizing processes is not new. What is new is (a) the global reach of these business, cultural, and military ideas and processes; (b) the capacity of promoters of globalizing militarism to wield lethal power; (c) the fact that so many private companies are now involved in this globalization of militarization; and (d) the intricacy of the international alliances among the players.

Asking feminist questions is a valuable means of understanding how and why *both* the globalization of militarization *and* the militarization of globalization happen. Posing feminist questions, furthermore, can help reveal the potential consequences of these processes for both women and men. Each of us probably has had the experience—with friends, with family, perhaps even with teachers—of insisting upon asking about things that others would much rather take for granted. They think you are a nuisance to be posing these questions:

> "Dad, how come on farms producing food for export it's usually the women who do the weeding?"
> "Well, because they always have. That's just the way it is! Anyway, what's the big deal about weeding?"

Of course, we might be the lazy ones. Other people might have to nudge us toward becoming curious. Perhaps we are the ones who don't want to be bothered asking new questions. It can be quite comfortable taking a lot of things for granted. That is why it takes so much effort by so many people to turn something most people take for granted—the fact that it is mainly women who weed, the fact that miners breathe in coal dust, the fact that many high school students join a military cadet corps, the fact that people become poorer as they grow older—into an *issue*.

Something becomes an "issue" only when a lot of people do two things: first, they start questioning it and stop taking it for granted, and second, they begin to believe it deserves public attention and public resolution. Persuading people to do both of these things is not easy. Since so many cultures and so many governments treat women's experiences as not worth exploring and create the impression that the condition of women is merely a private matter, converting any aspect of women's lives into an issue has taken—and still takes—enormous effort.

For instance, if a lot of people begin to be curious about why it is mainly women who weed, but they still stop short of calling for public responsibility for this situation, then the fact that it is mainly women who weed won't become an issue. However, even the emergence of just a popular curiosity about why women are designated as the weeders may, further down the road, provoke people to call for more public responsibility for the causes and consequences of that agricultural division of labor. They may start looking into the international politics of cotton, of strawberries, of coffee.

Creating a new curiosity is an important first step—and it's not so easy to take. But nothing can become an issue if the exercise of curiosity remains a private activity or if what you uncover is deemed unworthy of public response.

So it is tough to turn something into an issue. Issue making is a political activity. It requires developing a new curiosity plus spreading that curiosity among a lot of people in their roles as public citizens. Think of all the things that today are being treated nationally or internationally as issues, things that fifteen years ago were not considered "issues." When, for example, did male soldiers' use of women as prostitutes become an issue at least in a few countries? How about "stalking"? When did militaries' use of land mines become an issue? Becoming an issue is never automatic. Each issue's development has its own history. Each issue needs to be explained. Every issue has become an issue only because some people stopped taking it for granted, developed a new curiosity about it, and managed to persuade a lot of us who used to be complacent about it to become newly curious, too—and to start finding answers that made them think afresh about citizens' and governments' responsibilities for those dynamics that they had discovered.

Using a *feminist* curiosity is asking questions about the condition of women—and about relationships of women to each other and about relationships of women to men. It is also *not* taking for granted—thus it is insisting upon exploring—the relationships of women to families, to men, to companies, to movements, to institutions, to ideologies, to cultural expressions, to the state, and to globalizing trends.

Developing a *feminist* curiosity can be energizing. It motivates one to treat as puzzling the relationships of women to any aspect of social life and nature that other people take for granted. So many people in most societies usually say (and many of us said before we began to cultivate our own feminist curiosity) that we do not need to ask about the condition of women or assumptions about women because they are "natural" or because they are "trivial."

> "Mom, why do all these carmakers drape women models over their new automobiles?"
> "Oh, dear, don't worry. Nobody takes that seriously."

Beware the adjective "natural." Beware "trivial." Both are boulders rolled up against a door you may want to open. Rolling away those boulders can take a lot of intellectual and social stamina. Using a feminist curiosity, one discovers that who weeds is not "natural"; it flows from who is assigned to weed, which child is pulled out of school because a life of weeding won't require the ability to read and write. Who is assigned to weed may determine who in the village is not trained to operate a tractor. Who weeds may turn out to have a lot to do with who is not legally permitted to inherit land. Following the bread crumbs of these questions reveals that "Who weeds and who doesn't?" is not a trivial question to pursue. It is a question whose exploration can shed a bright light on globalized agriculture, on who benefits from it, and on who stays mired in poverty because of it.

Developing and using a feminist curiosity does take a lot of energy. Many of you might have sat in a class and felt hesitant to raise your hand to ask a question, sensing people around you letting out an audible sigh, "Oh, there she goes again." It takes energy to go ahead and ask that question, to not let a misleading assumption about women or about men, about boys or about girls just slide by. Continuing to pose feminist questions even takes a kind of courage.

"Thinking about your lecture about international terrorism, Professor, shouldn't we ask 'Where are the women?'"

Or: "Excuse me, sir, but in your discussion about nuclear trade policy, do you think that it matters to ask about international contests over masculinity?"

Exercising a feminist curiosity, therefore, is not a passive endeavor. It is not a quiet intellectual pastime. It is intellectual, but it takes stamina. And, I have become convinced, exercising a feminist curiosity calls on us to develop a kind of politics that has to be nurtured and cultivated; it does not just grow by itself. And for those who raise their eyebrows or utter an audible sigh or theatrically roll their eyes when a friend or colleague poses a feminist question— that raising of an eyebrow, letting out a sigh, or rolling one's eyes each is also a political act. Each of those gestures is meant to discredit, maybe even to silence, the feminist questioner. Each of those gestures is meant to keep the boulders firmly up against the door.

This book also calls on us to move beyond an interest in the *im-*

pacts of global affairs on women—though those impacts are important and do need careful monitoring. This book is a call to action, a call to use a feminist curiosity to develop explanations—that is, to discover *causes.*

"Move beyond impacts to causes." It sounds deceptively bland. Yet wielding a feminist curiosity, one finds that one is not just spelling out the impacts (consequences) of anything on women, but delving into whether pressuring women to act and believe in certain ways actually explains why something has occurred: the outbreaks and perpetuation of wars; the spread of certain industries from rich countries to poor countries; the continued abuse of the environment (yes, it could be that it will take a feminist curiosity to fully explain why those arctic ice caps are melting).

Explanation—the discovery of what causes what—is the "brass ring" of any analytical endeavor. If you can discover a cause for something, you are on your way to creating a theory about it. A *theory* is an explanation that is backed by specific publicly shared evidence. Moreover, an explanation does not rise to the status of a theory until it has been reliably tested.

Still, let's look for a moment at *impact* analysis. It requires curiosity, too. And getting a feminist curiosity onto the agenda when people at the table are choosing what questions will be asked about impacts—outcomes, consequences—can be a challenge. Ask anyone with a feminist curiosity who has worked for a corporation, a local government, an international agency, a humanitarian aide organization. "What will the U.S. government policy of requiring the teaching of sexual abstinence in order to qualify for reproductive health aid mean for girls' relationships to men in Uganda?" "What did sending thousands of male UN peacekeeping forces into East Timor mean for those Southeast Asian women?" Getting their colleagues to take seriously the weighing of the impacts on women of any action the group is about to take can be a frustrating endeavor.

Often, even if official pronouncements are made calling for the condition of women and the ideas of women to be taken seriously, the actual institutional response is merely a token response—that is, officials go through the superficial motions, but don't alter their masculinist practices and policy presumptions (e.g., they appoint a "gender advisor" to their department but starve that person of resources and leave that person out of the loop of crucial information flows needed to do the job effectively). This has happened in national militaries, corporate businesses, and international agencies. Thus, developing the finely honed skills to distinguish tokenism from genuine change is useful when dissecting both globalization and militarization.

A "gender impact analysis" is a new tool in local and global policymaking. Gender impact analysis should be—but is rarely—completed before any final decision is made; decisions such as allowing a new foreign company to come into one's region or country to open a new copper mine, signing an alliance with another government that entails building a new air force base, permitting a foreign film distribution company to buy up most of the country's movie theaters, and legalizing a new anti-AIDS drug call for asking:

- How will this decision (in contrast to the other options on the table) affect men? Which men especially?
- How will this affect women? Will it affect certain women more than other women?
- How will this policy choice affect the relationships between women and men? Will it shrink the inequalities? Widen the disparities? Globally or locally or both?

Gender impact analyses are difficult to do. It takes skills and training. Some professional schools are still refusing to incorporate this training into their curriculum, depriving their students of the skills they will need. Today, however, those gender-analysis skills are being taught in new graduate programs and special training programs all over the world. Networks of feminist scholars, women engaged in local women's groups, and feminist-informed agency staff members are meeting, for instance, in Canada, Thailand, and Kenya to write new gender-analysis training manuals and to create new courses to increase the number of people who have the skills to perform gender investigations and assessments of policy proposals. These gatherings don't make headlines, CNN crews don't arrive there with their cameras, but nevertheless, the people who travel across time zones to take part in these meetings are helping to globalize a feminist curiosity. Among the most effective globalized feminist networks are

- *Women Living Under Muslim Laws (WLUML)*, whose activists, themselves women from Muslim backgrounds, monitor and challenge nationalist discourses, religious intolerance, sexist laws, and sexist practices rationalized in the name of Islam and organize international campaigns to support local women subjected to patriarchal Islamist regimes;
- the *Women's International League for Peace and Freedom (WILPF)*, which was founded in The Hague in 1915, during World War I, by 1,300 women activists from Europe and North America who opposed this devastating war (one million men were killed or maimed in the stalemated muddy trench warfare in France in the five-month Battle of the Somme alone) and now has its headquarters in Geneva, with active branches in Sweden, Norway, Burundi, Sierra Leone, Canada, Russia, Japan, Australia, the United States, and other countries (Stiehm 2006);
- the *Women's Initiatives for Gender Justice*, a newer network of feminists pressuring the new International Criminal Court (established in 1999 as the first international war crimes court) to take explicit actions to ensure that systematic rape and sexual slavery in wartime are explicitly recognized and prosecuted as war crimes;
- *Women in Conflict Zones Network (WICZNET)*, which is coordinated from Canada and brings together women from the former Yugoslavia, Sri Lanka, Canada, and Britain who work in research institutions and international organizations, such as the International Committee of the Red Cross, UNICEF, and the UN High Commissioner for Refugees, as well as grassroots feminists, to shine light on the experiences and analyses of women living in war-torn regions (Giles, de Alwis, Klein, and Silva 2003);
- *Women Waging Peace*, which was first launched by a former U.S. ambassador who had seen firsthand both the impact of war on women in Bosnia during the early 1990s and local women's own courage and organizing skills, and has become a network designed to support and build bridges between often isolated local women's peace groups, among them groups in the Congo, Bosnia, Georgia, and Sierra Leone; and

14

- *Women in Black,* a network of women in countries around the world—in Israel, Serbia, Spain, Italy, Japan, the United States, Britain—who oppose militarism and its roots in patriarchy and nationalism and who hold silent vigils open to all women, standing prominently every week in their own city's busy intersections (Women in Black 2005; Cockburn forthcoming).

Two WILPF leaders have been awarded Nobel Peace Prizes (Jane Addams in 1931 and Emily Greene Balch in 1946). Women in Black's Belgrade and Jerusalem groups were nominated for the Nobel Peace Prize in the late 1990s.

All six of these globalizing feminist networks have made the exposing of, and the rolling back of, local and international militarist policies, ideas, and practices central to their work. Members of all six also have become convinced that, given the ways in which hydra-headed militarization works, the most effective actions are those that not only are sensitive to local cultures, politics, and priorities but also embrace international alliances in which to share ideas and information and to coordinate actions. Members of all six of these groups, furthermore, have become convinced that women have special roles to play in exposing and challenging militarization, *not* because women are somehow innately, biologically wired for peacefulness, but because women are so often outside the inner circles where militarizing decisions are being made yet are likely to be called upon to support, and even work on behalf of, militarizing agendas.

That is, members of all six groups, while they differ in their ways of organizing, their modes of resistance, and their country focuses, share a conviction that we must take women seriously *and* that it is crucial to challenge those particular ideas about masculinity, about femininity, and about patriarchal social orders that they have come to see as the local and global engines of militarization (Cockburn forthcoming; Hawkesworth 2006; Giles, de Alwis, Klein, and Silva 2003; Bauer and Helie 2006; Women in Black 2005; Spees 2003; Women Waging Peace and International Alert 2005).

Yet many international and national decision makers prefer to leave these new feminist analytical tools to rust in the basement. If the policy elites did use the gender analysis tools, they might have

15

to change their agendas. For example, if they commissioned gender impact analyses and then acted on their findings, officials in natural disaster relief agencies might have to significantly reallocate their resources. When planning for future tsunami, earthquake, or hurricane relief, many people (though not all, and not necessarily those with authority) have learned the hard way that it is always important to ask ahead of time about the likely impacts both on women and on men—of every economic class, of every ethnic group. Why? Because, of all the thousands of people who died in the giant waves set off by the December 2004 Indian Ocean tsunami, a majority turned out to be women and their dependent children. Likewise, in the chaotic aftermath of Hurricane Katrina, which devastated the Gulf Coast of the southern United States in September 2005, it was African American women and their dependent children who were especially endangered by the lack of government preparedness and the resultant overcrowding of unsanitary emergency shelters.

Look at another recent example of how a serious engagement with gender impact analysis would push officials to alter their political decisions. In 2005, the Iraqi and American male political elites who together hammered out Iraq's first post-Saddam constitution deliberately inserted (or passively allowed) provisions for putting much of family law—those laws determining marriage, divorce, child custody, and inheritance—under the influence of conservative male clerical officials. Some Iraqi women went into the streets in the summer of 2005 to protest. But these women's advocates weren't inside Baghdad's fortified, exclusive Green Zone where the U.S. administrators have their offices and where the constitutional deals and compromises were being made. These Iraqi women were certainly talking about gender impacts; they were convinced that inserting these conservative provisions into the new constitution would push most Iraqi women further out to the margins of the country's public life. But neither the American nor the Iraqi officials wielding the most influence in the constitutional process ordered a formal gender impact statement to be written or to be discussed in public or to be taken into serious account by senior negotiators. Iraqi women activists—and they grew in number as the war dragged on, despite the risks involved in being publicly visible as women as the violence escalated during 2005 and 2006—were shut out of high-level American and Iraqi elite policymaking. Iraqi women activists didn't lead any of the Iraqi political parties; they didn't control any U.S. or new Iraqi army or police regiments or the multiplying sectarian Iraqi militias; they didn't occupy the positions of clerics or of media editors. Those were the people being taken seriously, and they were virtually all male. The result: passage of a new constitution that many Iraqi women's rights advocates believed would undermine even the status women had under the former authoritarian regime.

Impacts matter. Wielding a feminist curiosity about impacts is a valuable analytical activity. When that feminist curiosity is not used there are real-life consequences.

So, when we weigh whether we need to "go beyond impacts to causes," what is being considered is *not* that we should stop posing gender impact questions. In fact, many women's rights advocates have urged that compulsory "gender impact studies" be included in the negotiating process by which every piece of legislation and every international agreement is hammered out. No hurricane prevention or relief plan should be approved, no constitution should be ratified, no foreign investment should be approved, no new military base agreement should be signed until there has been a thorough and public accounting of the potential impacts on women, on men, and on the relationships between women and men (equalizing or unequalizing). Yet when we "go beyond impacts to causes," we gain something more.

To make sense of today's complex world, we need to understand that many decisions have not only gendered *consequences* but gendered *causes*—that is, causes flowing from presumptions or fears about femininity or masculinity. It is only by using our feminist curiosity that we can expose these gendered causes. For instance, certain phrases do not merely have a destructive impact on certain women; the popularity of those phrases is *caused* in part by ideas about women, by presumptions about femininity and masculinity. Thanks to all the good colleagues around the world who have been educating me, I have learned that if one takes seriously the lives of women, if one pays close attention to the ideas, the histories, and the experiences of diverse women, one not only uncovers consequences but begins to uncover causality. Creating a feminist causal

17

analysis takes us to a deeper level of understanding of how and why the world "works" the way it does.

When you try to explain anything, you are seeking causality. Any explanation is an argument about causality. It calls for the gathering and the honest, careful weighing of credible evidence.

Thus, one of our newest feminist revelations is that one cannot explain why the international system works the way it does without taking women's lives seriously. "Experts" may be knowledgeable about banking interest rates, about the oil industry, about HIV/AIDS; nevertheless, if those experts fail to think seriously about women's lives, they are certain to produce a deeply flawed under-standing—explanation—of today's international political economy. An example: there is a rising awareness that HIV/AIDS is being spread because of armed conflicts. The simple causal explanation thus might be that "war causes AIDS." But feminist investigators have found that that level of causal explanation is just not adequate. After all, firing a gun doesn't spread the virus. Rather, these investi-gators have found, it is the increasing sexual violence by men—men armed with weapons and with masculinized arrogance and often ethnic or racial contempt—against girls and women in the midst of armed conflict that is causing the spread of the deadly virus.

Saying that taking women's lives seriously is necessary for devel-oping reliable explanations about much of what is going on in the world, including the interactions between militarizing change and globalizing change, is a radical feminist assertion. The term *radical* comes from the ancient word for *root*. So to say that this is a radical feminist assertion is to say that it is going to the root of how we understand militarized globalization or globalized militarization. It is an assertion that anybody who is interested in international poli-tics—a legislator, a journalist, a professor, an activist, your boss, or your best friend—but refuses to take women's lives seriously is going to be an unreliable guide into today's and tomorrow's interna-tional system.

True, this is a risky assertion to make. You should not just swal-low it. You can do your own evidence gathering, your own testing. Then, out of that exploring, you can reach your own thoughtful conclusions about whether this feminist causal assertion about how globalization and militarization work "holds water."

TRACKING THE MILITARIZED
GLOBAL SNEAKER

Let's start testing this feminist causal explanatory tool by looking at the international politics of factory work. If we consciously use a feminist curiosity, we can see how the promoters of globalizing factory work rely on manipulations of ideas about "femininity" and the "dutiful daughter." Their goal: to cheapen the cost of the labor needed to produce those globalized goods for export and company profit.

Those efforts to make—and keep—that labor cheap often become dependent on militarism. In other words, many of the sneakers that look white or blue or neon pink on the surface may turn out to be threaded with khaki on the inside.

"Cheap labor" is the work of some employees who are paid relatively little for their effort. The challenge for us is to question this commonly accepted (i.e., *unquestioned*) notion of "cheap labor" by using a feminist curiosity. This won't be easy because "cheap labor" is so commonly used to explain the increasingly globalized world we live in. The concept of "cheap labor" is offered to listeners and readers every day in media debates, in legislatures, and sometimes even in antiglobalization movements to explain why some regions or countries are more attractive to business investors than others:

"Oh, Company X is moving its factories to Asia because they're attracted by its cheap labor."

Or: "Sure, the Mexican government is going to win out over the Canadian government in attracting foreign investment because the Mexicans can offer companies cheap labor."

Women's labor is especially likely to be thought of as cheap. While men's labor—particularly the labor of men from ethnically and racially marginalized groups—can be thought of as cheap (think about the history of gold mining and the building of railroads), in the past 150 years it has been women's labor that has most often been imagined as allegedly "cheap," or worthy only of low pay. In globally competitive industries such as the textile industry, the garment industry, the shoe industry, the processed food industry, the electronics industry, and the toy industry, therefore, it has been women who have been deliberately hired to produce goods cheaply. Think "Barbie," ask about women's cheap labor; think computer chips, ask about women's cheap labor; think blue jeans, ask about women's cheap labor.

Staying uncurious while employing this easy phrase "cheap labor" depends on making the assumption that labor of women inevitably *is* cheap. It depends on making the deeper assumption that women's labor is "naturally" cheap, that women's labor is automatically cheap, that women's labor is cheap in a way that requires no policy decisions, no pressure, no manipulation. If we take for granted that women's labor is cheap labor, then we (students, civil servants, legislators, economists, activists, corporate executives) can comfortably move right ahead to build our corporate strategy or our international development plan on this unexplored assumption.

Now let's look at a radically different analytical possibility. Using a feminist curiosity, let's not accept an assumption, let's ask a question: is women's labor *made* cheap? As soon as you start using this new phrase—"women's labor *made* cheap"—you find yourself motivated to ask another new question: by whom?

Your curiosity now is being energized. You are inspired to ask even deeper questions. Digging deeper, you start asking: How? How is any woman's labor made cheap?

Now you are on an analytical roll. There is no dampening your

20

feminist curiosity. You have lots of new questions to pose about globalized (or local) women's factory work. Making—and keeping—women's labor "cheap" does not look so easy anymore. It looks as though it takes effort by myriad actors. And so the international practice of using women's skills, talents, attentiveness, and energies begins to seem more political, more dependent on the wielding of power—psychological, cultural, legal, economic, and (as we will see) maybe even militarized power—by various people and institutions. Militarized police being called in by employers and government officials to quell a labor demonstration organized by women factory workers who have decided that their labor should not be "cheap" is a common occurrence in this age of globalization.

The low wages paid to women working on an assembly line no longer look "natural." Anything that is described as "natural" thus should be carefully examined under the feminist curiosity microscope, because anything that is labeled "natural" is something you are being encouraged *not* to explain. If it is labeled "natural," allegedly, it took no effort to make it that way: "Today thousands of women in factories all over Asia stitch Nike sneakers. So what? What is interesting about that? Women stitch. Women have always stitched. Sewing, it's just what women naturally do."

Ha!

A little aside here: I grew up outside of New York City. I was a classic American postwar suburban teenager. When I was in middle school, all girls were required to take home economics—cooking, sewing, and hygiene. Of course, the boys went to separate classes where they were taught carpentry and car repair. We girls were taught how to scramble eggs and sew a hem. What I learned back then, long before I became a feminist, was that sewing is *not* a natural skill for all girls or for all women. In fact, it was so *unnatural* that it took the help of three of my mother's friends to get me through the sewing section of that home economics course. I was failing, so my splendid mother, who also did not sew, had to phone three of her suburban friends to help little Cynthia get a skirt sewn that would pass muster. Therefore, when you find a girl or a woman sewing, stitching at home or in a factory, you need to *explain* how she learned that skill, who decided it was a skill she (not her brother) should learn, and why. If it's not "natural," then it needs to be explained.

So the first assumption to investigate in any examination of women in globalized factory work is the assumption that the women in the factories are there because they are doing naturally what women always do. Who benefits from this widespread assumption? It will probably turn out to be an alliance of diverse beneficiaries: parents, boyfriends, government planners, local factory managers, foreign corporate executives, overseas retailers, and shoppers hoping for bargains.

This act of feminist curiosity will prompt you to be skeptical about three additional common assumptions that are made today by "experts" in international political economy: first, the assumption that no government official (in alliance with company executives) ever had to think about ways to put the women there on that factory floor; second, the assumption that no government official (or company executive) ever had to think about how to *keep* women there; and third, the assumption that no company executives ever had to sit around the table and devise strategies to create and sustain an alliance with local government officials for the sake of making (and keeping) women's pay low and their labor thereby "cheap." Three assumptions. Three failures of curiosity creating three dangerous analytical traps.

A *non*feminist investigator of globalized capitalism assumes that no corporate executives ever had to hold a serious business strategy session to figure out how to keep women's labor cheap. That same investigator of international capitalism also imagines—lazily—that no corporate manager ever had to strategize about how to work with local government officials in order to get the "kind" of women—or girls—they wanted: old or young? urban or rural? local or migrant? married or unmarried? ethnicity A or ethnicity B?

The analysts who make these lazy assumptions usually are not challenged by anyone. They are thus allowed—by their supervisors, by their clients, by us—to go on making these flawed assumptions about women who work in international trade. Unchallenged, they continue talking about "cheap labor." They continue to discuss globally competitive trade or export processing zones, *as if* their expert

22

understanding of international politics were rational, complete, reliable, and realistic.

It is not.

In reality, this widely used approach to the politics of global business, with its lack of a feminist curiosity, is too simplistic. It is an approach that hides power. Once you adopt a new questioning feminist curiosity, you begin to notice how many decisions, how many calculations, how many strategy changes it actually took to get those women into that factory. Suddenly you realize it took a lot more corporate and governmental thinking, the allocation of a lot more resources, and the wielding of a lot more power to get that woman to do (and to keep doing) the allegedly "natural" work she is doing—stitching a sneaker, assembling a microchip—for lower pay than the casual users of the phrase "cheap labor" have been willing to admit.

When I gave a talk in Tokyo a couple of years ago, I asked everyone in the audience to take off their shoes and to look at the labels inside to see where their shoes were made. I deliberately wore my sneakers that night. Professor Chizuko Ueno, the evening's discussant, and Professor Yumiko Mikanagi, our moderator, two well-known Japanese feminist scholars, both joined our collective investigation. We began with Professor Ueno. She found that though she'd purchased her fashionable, shiny black Reebok sneakers in New York, they had been made in the Philippines. Professor Ueno exclaimed, "So, actually I have caved in to exploitation!"

I tried to reassure her: "You have a lot of company. That is why I wore my sneakers tonight. I thought that I could not talk about how women's pay is made so low and pretend that I am not taking part in it too." My sneakers that night were New Balance—made in China. Others in the audience, doing research on their own shoes, started calling out the countries listed on the labels inside their shoes: "Brazil." "China." "China." "China." "Thailand." "Thailand." "Brazil." "Argentina." "Germany." "Japan." "China." "Thailand." "Indonesia." "Indonesia." "Vietnam."

In which of these countries have women been sewing these shoes with little right to create their own independent unions? In which of these countries do executives and government officials agree that using armed force to intimidate women labor organizers is necessary for company and national productivity? In which of these

23

countries are women persuaded that they don't deserve promotions because they will be quitting paid work once they get married and become unpaid housewives? In which of these countries are women employees afraid to demand better working conditions (e.g., less forced overtime) because they believe their primary duty as good daughters is to keep sending money home to their impoverished rural parents?

That is, there are questions to ask, country by country, company by company. One shouldn't assume that every company or every country is identical, even if they share broad similarities. Curiosity is crucial. Close attention to women factory workers and their relationships to their parents, to their fellow women workers, to their boyfriends or husbands, to their managers, to their government officials, and to foreign corporate executives thousands of miles away is called for.

Here is another research report "from the field." While still in Tokyo, I started going into the brightly lit sneaker shops along Tokyo's busy Takeshita Street. Here are my informal research findings: Converse low-top sneakers—so popular today in Japan and the United States—now are being made by women in Indonesia. Converse was recently bought by Nike but still markets its own distinctive styles. You can conduct your own research by reading sneaker labels in shops near you—in Durham or San Diego, in Leeds or London, in Santiago or St. Louis.

Style is political. In today's highly competitive globalized sneaker industry, the more elaborate the stitching, the more incentive corporate executives have to *make* the stitchers' labor "cheap." For example, envision the popular, multicolored Converse low-tops. They are among the least fancy of sneakers. "Hip," yes, but not fancy in either their materials or their stitching. Compare those low-tops now with the sneakers favored by soccer or basketball stars and the shoppers who admire their style. The fancier the stitching, the more necessary it will be for a sneaker executive to keep the stitchers' wages low in order to keep profits high. The more pressure factory managers and their corporate clients feel to keep the wages they pay their female workers low, the more tempting it will be for those same managers and corporate clients to tolerate militarized intimidation of their workers. Highly styled, complexly stitched sneakers—those sneakers for export whose profits depend on keeping workers unorganized—are more likely to carry a militarized price tag.

It was largely because the low-tops were designed with so little stitching that Converse kept its low-top factories in the United States, primarily in North Carolina, until recently. Although Converse executives decided to produce these low-tops in the United States, where wages are generally higher and safety regulations are generally more demanding, they chose a state whose local lawmakers have given local factory workers only limited rights to organize labor unions. Furthermore, Converse's own personnel officers seemed (we do not know this for sure because no one has yet done a gender and racial study of a Converse factory in the United States) to prefer African American women factory workers. These are women who, due to North Carolina's longtime racialized gender politics, have limited job opportunities and thus have been least able to protest their low wages.

But my research along Tokyo's bustling Takeshita Street revealed that Converse executives based in Andover, Massachusetts, recently changed their gendered global strategy. They moved their low-top sneaker production from North Carolina to Indonesia. Why? Was it just a calculation of kilometers? Indonesia is closer to Japanese teenage shoppers than is North Carolina. Or did the women working in Converse's North Carolina factories start organizing? And what gendered sales pitch did the Converse executives back in the United States hear from Indonesia's male government officials? What gendered message about Indonesian women did Converse strategists hear from rival sneaker makers already manufacturing in Indonesia that made the labor of *Indonesian women* seem so economically and politically appealing?

In 2003, Nike bought Converse. There was some speculation that Nike, known worldwide for its very intricate sneaker designs—designs dependent on elaborate and complicated stitching by its Asian women employees—would push Converse to abandon its simple styles. But three years later, Nike's executives decided to keep the traditional styles because Converse sales were rising, as young consumers from Tokyo to Oslo, London to Chicago adopted the multicolored low-tops and high-tops as their symbols of counterculture (Kang 2006). Young sneaker buyers were wearing Con-

25

verse to announce that they were off the Nike global fashion grid, perhaps not realizing that Nike now was banking the profits of their Converse purchases.

The corporate decision makers of New Balance, headquartered in Boston (my current hometown), adopted a different feminized (reliant on women) geographic strategy. Until four or five years ago, New Balance executives marketed their global brand as "made in the USA," hiring mainly new immigrant women living in the Boston area to stitch their sneakers. They seemed to think that consumers would view New Balance as a more socially responsible company if they kept producing their sneakers in a country and a region that allowed its mainly female workforce to unionize. This practice also allowed the mail-order retailer L.L.Bean to feature New Balance sneakers in their popular catalogs with a good conscience. But since 2000, New Balance can no longer make that claim. New Balance executives moved most of their manufacturing operations from Boston to China and Vietnam. Hoping consumers will understand, New Balance now inserts a card into each sneaker box explaining that they try to produce as many of their sneakers in the United States as possible.

Dates matter. Historical development matters. Gendered uses of power, which push certain women to stitch sneakers in certain countries more than in others, are not stagnant. A feminist curiosity is a historically lively curiosity. With a feminist curiosity, one keeps track of diverse women and ideas about diverse women around the world over time. The gendered global politics of sneakers—like all forms of gendered international politics—therefore has to be historicized.

So, open your closet and look at all your shoes. Now line up all your sneakers according to the year in which you think they were made. Borrow your mother's and father's oldest pairs of sneakers, too, so that you will have a longer historical time line to work with. You will be prompted now to start asking feminist questions about the time-specific dynamics of women's labor, women's hopes, women's organizing, governments' competing industrial policies, and corporate executives' changing geographic calculations about how to make women's labor cheap.

The recent history of South Korean women working in sneaker

factories makes this clear. According to investigations by women's studies researcher Seung-Kyung Kim, executives of American, European, and Japanese sneaker companies and electronics companies were deliberately wooed, starting in the 1960s, by South Korea's then-military government led by the authoritarian president Chung Hee Park, who was eager to achieve rapid industrialization and compete in the emerging global economy (1997). In crafting their strategy, General Park and his military and civilian economic advisors did not rely on the widespread flawed assumption that it was "natural" for Korean women to stitch sneakers or to assemble delicate electronics products. These economic-policy strategists did, however, assume that women—especially young women—would be better stitchers than their Korean brothers. But they realized that sewing in their parents' homes and sewing in a Nike factory were very different ideologically. Thus, in the 1960s and early 1970s, the military government of Chung Hee Park launched a calculated campaign to change Korean citizens' image of the "respectable" Korean young woman. Conflating the concepts of "national security," "national pride," "modernization," and "industrial growth," this military government set about to persuade the parents of daughters to radically alter their own definitions of what was "natural" for "decent" ("marriageable") South Korean young women to do outside their homes. The government's campaigners argued that a young unmarried woman who stitched, not under her parents' careful supervision, but instead under the supervision of a foreman in a factory miles away from home, could be endowed with a "respectable" femininity and an appealing feminized morality that would still make her attractive on the Korean marriage market.

Nike, Reebok, and Adidas could not be lured to South Korean factories in the 1960s and 1970s *unless* the Park regime could transform Korean parents' ideas about what is "natural" and what is "respectable" behavior for "dutiful daughters." If we are not curious about mothers' and fathers' changed ideas of daughterhood, respectability, and marriageability, we will become *un*reliable analysts of the "Korean economic miracle."

So now dig deeper back into your family's closet. Pull out your oldest, most worn-out sneakers. If you can excavate a pair from the 1960s or early 1980s, most likely you will discover that the label says "made in Korea." Behind that label is a lot more decision making and a lot more power wielding than nonfeminist analysts imagine. For behind that label is an entire state ideological campaign to alter citizens' definitions of "femininity," and "feminine respectability." The state's goal: to make young, unmarried South Korean women's "daughterly" labor available—cheaply—to foreign corporations.

Nike was the first sneaker company to shed its own factories and to start relying on subcontractors to own and to manage the factories producing Nike sneakers. Consequently, the Korean young women mobilized in the 1960s and 1970s to work as patriotic dutiful daughters in sneaker factories were not hired—or fired—directly by Nike. They were hired, disciplined, paid, and fired by the Korean male entrepreneurs with whom Nike signed contracts. The masculinized sneaker company executives from the United States and Europe were in part attracted by the fact that many of these factory-owning Korean men—subcontractors for Nike and later for Reebok and Adidas—enjoyed close political relationships with the militarized South Korean political elite. No matter what bright color sneakers had on the outside, by the 1970s sneakers were turning a distinctive shade of khaki underneath.

Threaded through virtually every sneaker you own is some relationship to masculinized militaries. Locating factories in South Korea was a good strategic decision in the eyes of those Oregon-headquartered male Nike executives because of the close alliance between male policymakers in Washington and Seoul. It was a relationship—unequal but intimate—based on their shared anticommunism, their shared commitment to waging the Cold War, and their shared participation in an ambitious international military alliance.

Pusan, a major Korean port and industrial city, became, by the late 1970s, the "sneaker capital of the world." By then, other sneaker companies had copied the Nike model. Here are the key elements of this globalizing industrial model that made Pusan so central to the world's sneaker industry: (1) close the company's own factories; (2) put the women employees who make the sneakers at arm's length by hiring local male subcontractors to run the factories and to make cozy alliances with the local male political elites; (3) view shared anticommunist ideologies as good for profitable manufacturing; (4)

take comfort in a Cold War military alliance, as imagined by the U.S.-based company executives between "your" government and "their" government; (5) design corporate strategies to exploit local sexist ideas about femininity in order to justify low wages paid to young women workers; (6) depend on the local regime to craft a national ideology of "feminine respectability" that will enable your subcontractors to have a seemingly endless line of willing and unorganized women workers; (7) encourage consumers—women and men—in Japan, the United States, and Europe to imagine that *they* are "empowered" when they purchase and wear your high-priced sneakers; and (8) persuade these same consumers *not* to be curious about whether the Asian women stitching their sneakers also feel "empowered" when they go to work in Pusan's modern factories.

Any investigator of global political economy (or "development") who lacks a feminist curiosity will not even see half of the building blocks it has taken to create and sustain this popular formula.

This potent international formula was crafted in the 1960s and 1970s and continued to "work" for South Korean and U.S. and European policymakers into the mid-1980s. Despite significant changes in South Korea's political culture, especially the rise of a lively civil society, many elements of this gendered—militarized— neoliberal industrial formula still operate today in the early 2000s. To tell whether—and why—any elements of this global sneaker industry formula have genuinely changed requires curiosity about the politics (local, national, and international) of both femininity and masculinity. Here is just a sampling of some feminist questions we need to find the answers to:

- To what extent do Nike's American male executives and their Korean (or Indonesian or Chinese or Vietnamese) male factory managers (subcontractors) use their shared masculinity to build trust between each other in what is a highly stressful global economic climate?
- Do today's Indonesian, Vietnamese, and Chinese women sneaker workers all have identical ideas about being "feminine" or being "dutiful daughters"?
- Do Chinese, Korean, Vietnamese, and Indonesian government officials promote the same feminized idea about the "model woman worker"?

29

In the early 1980s, a prodemocracy movement gathered steam in South Korea. Its chief goal was to force the twenty-year-old military-centered regime to turn over power to a popularly elected civilian government. At the outset of the movement, students at prestigious Korean universities provided the ideas, leadership, and members. But soon women and men working in factories began to take part. Participation in any prodemocracy movement is gendered—the risks taken, the nature of the consciousness change, the sorts of political influence gained and the goals set by the movement, as well as the rewards, are likely to be different for (and thus differently weighed by) women and men. Again, feminist researcher Seung-Kyung Kim (1997) provides us with insights into these often-ignored gendered realities of a prodemocracy movement's evolution. Many thousands of South Korean women working in sneaker, electronics, and garment factories in the early to mid-1980s began to imagine something new: that when they were working in these factories, they were acting as citizens. They began to believe that they—as low-paid factory workers—were not just "dutiful daughters," they were not just future wives; they were *citizens*.

How do companies and governments keep any woman's labor "cheap"? Policymakers encourage that woman to imagine that she is not a citizen when she is in the factory working those long hours, stitching Nikes and Reeboks on the assembly line, but rather a dutiful daughter. Dutiful daughters obey supervisors; dutiful daughters think first of their parents' needs (and of their brothers' needs) and second about saving money for a future husband.

Therefore, if enough women on the sneaker assembly line begin to imagine that, as they stitch Nike sneakers, they are doing it not as dutiful daughters but as full citizens—that is, individuals invested with rights—policymakers in corporate and government offices are going to have a harder time keeping the labor of women "cheap." In European and North American countries, as well as in Asian, Middle Eastern, Latin American, and African countries, whole political cultures and legal systems have been cultivated over generations to discourage women from thinking of themselves as citizens. The reason it took decades of women's gutsy organizing to simply win the right to vote was that the men who ran governments, schools, newspapers, and churches stubbornly clutched onto the masculinist idea that the proper place for women was in the home, imagining them first and foremost as wives, daughters, or mothers, not as citizens (even if, in reality, many women were working in fields, in textile and garment factories, and in the kitchens and laundry rooms of wealthier people's homes). So the claim that they were citizens when they were sewing high-priced sneakers for export, not just daughters or would-be wives, was not a claim unique to Korean women workers. It was a claim that had to be developed and asserted by women in most countries.

Despite the risks, many South Korean women workers—though not all—did develop a new consciousness during the upheavals of the mid-1980s. It was this change in factory women's sense of who they were that then enabled a student-led prodemocracy movement to burst out of its own narrow middle-class confines and make alliances with working-class women and men.

We cannot just note this transformation that was to alter the global politics of the sneaker industry and then move on. We need to *explain* it. And that can be accomplished only using a feminist curiosity. Without posing serious feminist questions, we will fail to adequately explain the success of the historic South Korean prodemocracy movement of the 1980s. Furthermore, if we don't look closely at the hopes, dreams, skills, fears, and strategies of these Korean women working in sneaker (and electronics and garment) factories, we will fail to see the causal connections between the ouster of the Seoul generals and the departure of Nike from Pusan. We will fail to see that individual women's rethinking of "respectable femininity," and "daughterhood" and their reimagining of themselves as "citizens" not only can bring down state regimes but can alter the calculus on which contemporary international political economies rely. A citizen-worker is no longer an easily cheapened worker. One might try to picture conversations in Nike's Oregon headquarters in the mid-1980s as so many South Korean women struggled to see themselves as citizens: "Get out the map, Charlie, we're packing up in Pusan. Where is Jakarta?"

There was an opportunity in the late 1980s for the sneaker industry to remain globalized and feminized (reliant on women's assembly work) but become less militarized. If Nike and the other international sneaker companies had decided that the ouster of the generals and the success of the prodemocracy movement was "good for business" and thus stayed in Pusan, the sneaker industry would have remained global—headquarters in one country, factory managers and assembly workers in another country, and customers buying their products around the world—but it would have adapted to South Korea's new partially demilitarized political culture and relationships (including the newly energized labor movement and the increasingly vibrant women's movement). But that was not the decision that the sneaker executives headquartered in the United States and Europe made. They had gotten used to the business advantages offered by a militarized regime. If South Korea was going to roll back its own militarization even somewhat (not completely, as many Korean antimilitarist analysts are quick to point out), then the sneaker companies would move to another country where militarized politics were still entrenched. Indonesia looked appealing.

Capitalism (local and global) is not just about modernity. The architects of late-twentieth- and early-twenty-first-century capitalism have deliberately decided to exploit a false notion of tradition. In practice, this has proved a very tricky game to play. It takes clever footwork by state and company strategists to promote a capitalist brand of modernity by entrenching traditional daughterhood and traditional wifehood. Reread this previous sentence. Slow down when you get to "by." "By" is the strategic "trick" here. One might think this "by" is easy to accomplish, that it's quite simple to entrench traditional ideas and practices of daughterhood and wifehood—or one might imagine that these overseas-investing capitalists are just in a muddle. Not so. Patriarchy routinely tries to hide its confusion. One of the tasks of researchers is to pull back the curtain of alleged coherence and rationality to reveal the confusion operating just behind it. How that modernizing patriarchal capitalist confusion—evidenced by contradictions, mixed messages, ambivalence—is superficially rationalized and disguised is a question for any analyst who seeks to make sense of the contemporary international political economy. Thus we need to investigate both government officials' and company executives' mixed messages about daughters and marriage and simultaneously pay careful attention to girls' and women's own efforts to untangle and use these mixed messages. We have to craft the feminist curiosity and feminist skills to do both, because it is the dynamic intertwining of the two that helps shape what the globalized sneaker industry is today and what it is soon to become. We dare not be satisfied with a single still photograph. And we dare not let our attention wander.

In the late 1980s a major migration of an entire industry occurred. In search of the next population of "dutiful daughter" employees (in the name of industrial modernity)—and of a regime that would use its own authority to promote a revised "traditional" ideology of dutiful daughterhood—Nike, Reebok, Adidas, and other sneaker companies moved to Indonesia. They brought their Korean male factory-owning subcontractors with them, too. Indonesia's president was then General Suharto, head of a "New Order" militarized regime. Like General Chung Hee Park of South Korea twenty years earlier, General Suharto and his Indonesian male civilian economists, in pursuit of rapid industrialization fueled by foreign investment, set about to modernize the Indonesian idea of a respectable, dutiful daughter, though perhaps the Suharto officials took less initiative, instead following the lead of the foreign investors and their factory managers, who had their own clear ideas of what was "men's work" and what was "women's work" (Caraway forthcoming). Once again, with the aid of the popular media, mothers and fathers were convinced that letting a daughter move away from home to work in a sneaker (or electronics or garment) factory would not compromise that daughter's respectability or jeopardize her chances for a decent marriage.

By 2000, Nike and other global sneaker companies had (through their subcontractors) hired 100,000 Indonesian women employees. The government's military and the militarized police have helped keep these thousands of Indonesian young women unorganized and therefore their labor "cheap." The Indonesians' nationwide prodemocracy movement did not end this practice. But it hasn't just been the military. It has taken a complex, often unstable, combination of myths about "traditional Indonesian femininity" and media journalists' and editors' narratives, along with personal dreams of achieving a "good marriage," individual strategies for sustaining one's reputation as a "respectable woman," and state militarism to keep Indonesian sneaker workers' labor cheap. Just like the sneakers made in

South Korea in the 1970s, sneakers being produced today in Indonesia may be threaded with militarism.

When any government calls in security forces to put down labor protests by women sneaker workers (protests for decent wages, for the right to organize, for the end of forced overtime, for the end of sexual harassment by male supervisors), there is a gendered politics going on—on all sides. It is not just the women workers who are gendered. The men in the police and army who confront them with shields and batons and guns are also gendered insofar as they see their wielding of instruments of intimidation as expressions of their own manliness. In other words, whenever women workers are confronted by male security forces, we are witnessing feminized labor being deliberately intimidated with masculinized force. We need to direct our feminist curiosities *both* to the women working in the factories *and* to the uniformed men ordered by the government to keep them in line. At present, we know startlingly little about how these security forces and how these women experience—and strategize about—these sharply gendered confrontations at the sneaker factory gates.

So now, as the major sneaker companies—and their subcontractors—open scores of factories in Vietnam, Thailand, and China, we need to apply the same feminist curiosity to understand the extent to which current practices differ from the "model" created in Korea and the extent to which they are still the same. We need to make lists of what has changed and what has persisted. Neither Vietnam nor China has an overtly military regime in power, though each is governed by an authoritarian one-party regime. Until mid-2006, Thailand had a multiparty civilian government, but it was taken over by the military acting, it said, to end the rule of a corrupt and authoritarian civilian elected administration. All three countries have strong masculinized police and military forces that are deployed against their own citizens in the name of public order and national security. All three of these governments, while religiously diverse, are male dominated. And all three governments have attracted foreign investors by offering to mobilize millions of young women from rural villages to work miles away from home in new export factories. Is it pure oppression and intimidation that is making women's labor "cheap" in Vietnam, Thailand, and China, as well as in Indonesia? Or is it official intimidation and corporate profit strategizing combined with the government's manipulation of, and women's own evolving ideas about, femininity and marriage?

Before one imagines that there is no alternative to this widely entrenched system for making and keeping women sneaker workers' labor "cheap," it is worth looking at a small but imaginative experiment: a private company called No Sweat. On the company's website the owners state their philosophy concerning globalization:

> We believe that the only viable response to globalization is a global labor movement. No Sweat defines the market for goods that support independent trade unions—the only historically proven solution to sweatshops (No Sweat)

And printed inside each No Sweat sneaker is the company's motto: "100% union made."

The company was founded in 2004 by Jeff Ballinger, an American labor rights consultant and monitor, together with three others. For years, Ballinger had been charting the practices of the sneaker industry, especially the use of factories in Indonesia. During the 1990s, while the Suharto regime was still in power, Ballinger regularly published a four-page newsletter exposing the labor practices used in Indonesian sneaker factories to keep women's labor "cheap." He called his modest publication *Nike in Indonesia*. Gradually, this slim newsletter made its way into the hands of American op-ed journalists and even of Gary Trudeau, the politically minded cartoonist whose "Doonesbury" strip appears in newspapers across the United States. Nike executives began to feel pressure from consumers. Even some of their highly paid sports-star endorsers became defensive when asked why they were supporting exploitive labor practices.

Then came the 1998 prodemocracy movement in Indonesia, which toppled the Suharto regime. Regime change did not instantly lead to better working conditions for Indonesian women sneaker workers. But the political system opened up enough to permit some local labor unions to become more assertive on behalf of workers and to stop functioning merely as passive instruments of the government.

It was in this new less militarized political climate that Ballinger and his partners decided to launch No Sweat. They stayed in Indonesia. They were committed to proving that it was possible to create non-exploitation-reliant sneakers in Indonesia. They used their familiarity with the country's shoe business and relied on help from Indonesian labor advocates to compare factories. Were there any factories whose managers and owners were producing shoes without exploiting their workers? They finally decided on a factory owned by Bata, one of the world's biggest shoe manufacturers. They determined that Bata, which had a multigenerational history of paternalistic policies toward its employees, allowed their largely female workforce to join an autonomous labor union. That was No Sweat's core criterion. They also determined that Bata would provide workers stitching No Sweat's classic low-top black-and-white and red-and-white sneakers with decent, livable wages and employee benefits.

No Sweat inserts into each of its sneaker boxes a card summarizing the pay and benefits its Indonesian workers receive. For instance:

> Hospitalization: Employee—100 percent coverage; Family—100 percent onsite, 80 percent offsite
> Maternity (for female employee or wife of a male employee)— first child—225 rupees; second child—200 rupees; third child—150 rupees
> Shift allowance: first and second shifts—175 rupees per hour; third shift (night shift)—200 rupees per hour
> Working clothes (leather and canvas): two pairs per employee
> Rice allowance: 30 liters per month
> Ramadan bonus (most Indonesian employees are Muslim): eight weeks' salary.
> Pension: 3 percent contribution by the employee; 7 percent by the company.

This does not mean that there is no room for exercising a feminist curiosity about this small innovative experiment in alternative sneaker globalization. Jeff Ballinger himself is candid about the limitations of the Bata/No Sweat labor union, SPSI, to which their employees belong. In the past many of the male leaders of Indonesian labor unions have been more eager to protect male workers' benefits than to extend those of women workers, often seeing women workers as a threat to their male members' wages because they imagined factory managers were enamored with the strategy of substituting women for men in certain assembly line jobs where they could pay women less (Caraway forthcoming). This perception of women workers as a threat to male workers' pay rates has been commonplace among all too many male union leaders in many countries. Ballinger gives credit, however, to the activists inside the SPSI's Women's Bureau, an office created by women union members to focus especially on women workers' concerns and to monitor the union leaders' attentiveness to those concerns, for working against corruption and oppression and working for a decent national minimum wage. It is the combination of Bata's particular corporate philosophy, the evolving democratizing culture in post-Suharto Indonesia, and the work of SPSI's own women activists that has made No Sweat's anti-cheap-labor global business experiment possible. Using a feminist curiosity, we still need to know what the women stitching these No Sweat sneakers think about their working conditions and their union membership: do they feel as though the large national union's leaders are paying enough attention to their concerns? And we need to know more about whether working in a factory with such relatively good benefits and pay has altered these women's relationships with their parents, their brothers, their boyfriends, the police, the military, and Indonesia's civilian government officials. If in fact this anti-cheap-labor experiment has brought about meaningful change, then the relationships experienced by these women should be different from those experienced by their counterparts stitching sneakers in a Nike or Adidas factory across town.

Furthermore, as innovative as the No Sweat experiment is, it needs to be watched over time, just as the practices of sneaker companies, and women's responses to those practices, have to be watched over time. If faced with growing international competition, will Bata's managers, in whom the No Sweat owners have placed their trust, be tempted to cut back on the pension plan or on maternity leave? In the future, might some of the women stitching No Sweat sneakers begin to find the union too timid or too male domi-

37

nated and seek to switch their membership to a more assertive labor union?

Neither globalization nor militarization is an inevitable process. Each can be stalled or even occasionally reversed. This is why using a feminist curiosity takes stamina. One has to stay attentive.

Delving into the globalized and often-militarized evolution of the production politics of just one product, the sneaker, has shown us that we have to direct our curiosities to more than simply business and the state governments. We need to demonstrate how difficult it is to construct—and sustain—a kind of femininity that allows women's hard work to be cheapened, a kind of femininity that serves both corporate profit and a masculinized state development strategy. Fashioning and deploying an energetic feminist curiosity will enable us to pose those questions with which we can reveal the confusion hidden behind the patriarchy's facade of rationality, as well as the calculation and coercion that is required to get one woman to accept low wages and meager benefits in exchange for stitching one pair of globalized sneakers.

HOW DOES "NATIONAL SECURITY" BECOME MILITARIZED?

Many of the actions that serve to globalize militarization—that is, that spread the rationales and activities underpinning militarism—are, surprisingly, taken not in the name of international security but in the pursuit of *national* security. For instance, a government that calls upon its security forces to put down a workers' protest in an export factory might not claim that the workers' organizing is jeopardizing international security, but that it is undermining the nation's security. Similarly, a country may join (or take the lead in creating) an international military alliance—taking part in joint military maneuvers, standardizing weaponry and procedures, buying each other's fighter aircraft, pledging to come to each other's defense, sharing secrets—all in the name of enhancing its national security. Nonetheless, the creation and operation of such intercountry alliances can globalize militarism.

That is, national security and the globalization of militarization need to be considered together. The effect of some government decisions is not only to militarize one country's national security but also to militarize global politics—sometimes this effect is intentional, other times merely inadvertent.

Following World War II, the study of national security became a common fixture in the curricula of many universities, military academies, and civilian schools of diplomacy around the world. "National security" was widely viewed as encompassing a government's military operations and alliances, as well as the underlying foreign policy doctrines and strategies—even if civilian officials were in charge of such matters.

Complementing this particular understanding of national security has been a widespread assumption about what sorts of people make national security experts. It has been imagined that anyone wanting to be taken seriously in the field of national security—in government agencies, in think tanks, in graduate schools—has to be "rational." The opposite of rational has been imagined to be "emotional." This conventional assumption—combined with the common belief that "manly" men are the most rational beings, while less manly men and virtually all women are prone to being "emotional"—has made a certain kind of masculinity the entry ticket into national security discussions. National security thinking (including taking part in often fierce debates among national security experts) has been portrayed as leaving no room for sentimentality: one has to be able to confront unpleasant facts "without blinking"; one has to be "hard nosed." Rational manly security experts must be capable of "muscular thinking"; they must never show themselves to be "soft."

Thus, how one thinks about national security not only affects global relations but determines who is even allowed to sit at the table to take part in the security conversation. The more militarized the understanding of what national security is (and what it is not), the more likely it will be that the conversation about national security—and international security—will be a largely masculinized affair (Tickner 2001; Sjoberg and Tickner forthcoming). Certainly a handful of women might be allowed in now and then, but they will have to be constantly on their guard. They will have to make sure that they never appear (in the eyes of their colleagues) to be sentimental, emotional, or "soft"—that is, "feminine." And even many men will, under these restrictive conditions, have to be wary: if they betray emotion when they talk about the use of military force, they might risk forfeiting their masculine credentials, which in turn could mean being shut out of top-level discussions of national security.

Anything can be defined as a threat to national security, using the conventional understanding of that term, insofar as it appears to threaten the strength of the state. Thus, not just a foreign military mobilizing on the state's borders, but enemies far away believed to be planning to undermine the state by devious means may be viewed as threats to national security. Still other threats to national security can be seen close to home, posed by those inside the state. Most commonly, these people are labeled as subversives. During the 1950s, in what today is looked back upon as the "McCarthy era," those Americans labeled "subversives" included Communists, Communist sympathizers (broadly defined), and homosexuals.

In Third World, postcolonial societies in the 1960s to 1990s, threats to national (state) security also could include those women who were having "too many" children. The "population control" movement became a global movement, engaging scores of economists, demographers, development experts, and pharmaceutical companies (Hartmann 1995). Women were portrayed as being a threat. Or rather, women's "fertility," if left uncontrolled, was thought of as a threat—a threat to the country's economic stability and thus, allegedly, to the state's viability. Since instability in countries such as the Philippines, Kenya, India, Bangladesh, and China was viewed as exacerbating tensions in an already-fraught Cold War world, population control programs began to merge with militarized international calculations. Population control was a surprisingly masculinized global campaign (Hartmann 1995). Although men as sexual partners were left almost undiscussed and women of child-bearing age were made the prime target of these programs, it was men who did most of the official worrying, scientific research, pharmaceutical promotions, and strategizing. While millions of dollars and thousands of person-hours were spent trying to control women's fertility—to get women to have fewer children—women themselves were hardly deemed national security authorities.

Then came "Cairo." It became a turning point in the security-focused international politics of population. Cairo, Egypt, was the site for the large UN-sponsored 1994 conference on population, which brought to that city experts and government officials from dozens of countries—some from the countries posing a "population problem," some from the countries providing money to and directing projects in those other countries with the goal of enhancing their security. But something had changed. Women's advocates—

some calling themselves specialists in "women and development," others thinking of themselves as "women's rights" activists, still others openly taking on the label "feminist"—had learned the ways of the United Nations and the development bureaucracies of their own governments. These women's advocates had seen what happened to poor women when they were mere objects of population-control projects. The advocates had developed international alliances and networks to push for women's health, women's political empowerment, and what many activists now called "women's environmental security," as well as women's economic independence, and most innovatively, women's sexual autonomy. They succeeded in persuading the United Nations and the major governments orchestrating the 1994 Cairo meeting to call this conference *not* a conference on "population control" but instead the International Conference on Population and Development. In so doing, they forced a shift from a narrow, state-centered notion of security to a broader, more human-centered notion of security. Once the conference got underway in Cairo, these women from myriad countries—some rich, many poor—persuaded a majority of governments to publicly declare their understanding that anxieties about "population control" had to take a backseat to concerns for women's and girls' health and education. Moreover, women hereafter had to be treated as actors in the development and security-creating policy and implementation process—actors with rights over their own bodies. Since the Cairo conference of 1994, certain administrations in some countries (notably those of the Vatican and of the United States in the early 2000s) have tried to undercut this Cairo global consensus. Nonetheless, after the Cairo conference, the international security discourse on population changed (Eager 2004). It was no longer taken for granted that women's fertility could be reduced to a security issue for states, and more women concerned about the lives of women were actively engaged in the designing of health and economic, as well as environmental and foreign policy, research and the crafting of the policies often flowing from this research.

In recent years, particularly since the end of the Cold War, which brought with it the termination of the great power rivalry between the United States and its allies on the one hand and the Soviet Union and its allies on the other (with many other less powerful countries left to carve out precarious spaces somewhere in the volatile middle between the behemoths), there has been a flood of fresh thinking about security.

More questions are being posed these days about whose security should be prioritized. Some are asking what the difference is between "national" and "state" security. Is "human security" a more valuable way to conceptualize genuine security pursuits? People asking this question are suggesting that security is more likely to be realistically assessed and pursued if less emphasis is put on governments and their military capacities and more attention is paid to the needs that must be fulfilled for ordinary individuals to experience genuine security. For instance, maybe taking stronger action to stop global warming, to provide clean water worldwide, and to prevent the further spread of HIV/AIDS would move us closer to achieving meaningful global security than would investing so much energy and public money in developing fighter planes and recruiting millions of young people into state military forces (Basch 2005; Hoogensen and Stuvoy 2006).

Not everyone is convinced that human security is the most effective way of achieving national security, however. In most countries the government-centered, militarized version of national security remains the dominant mode of policy thinking, even if today it is being challenged.

This post–Cold War era was taking shape in the 1990s at the very same time that feminist scholarship investigating the complex workings of international affairs was beginning to make itself felt inside academia and international agencies. This development was the product of years of researching, teaching, and organizing. The reason that women are now considered important actors in measuring and pursuing alternative forms of less militarized "security" is that this feminist work had been done.

So, as we now plunge into a discussion of national security—how it has been militarized and how it might be demilitarized—it is worth spending a bit of time here to look inside one academic organization where this development of alternative security thinking has gained prominence. Scholarly organizations—for example, the American Historical Association, the International Studies Association, the British International Studies Association, the Association for Asian Studies, the National Women's Studies Association, the American Political Science Association, the Modern Language Association, the Middle East Studies Association—may seem quite remote from the lives and studies of undergraduate students. But often, unbeknownst to students, these associations influence decisions about who earns a doctoral degree (and who is discouraged), what books and articles get published and assigned for courses, what sorts of topics are taken seriously in classrooms (and what topics get only minimal attention in a semester's syllabus), and what new interdisciplinary programs and majors are launched.

The International Studies Association is not one of the largest academic associations, yet it has been the principal forum in which both long-standing and new ideas about how to investigate and teach global affairs are compared and tested. While English remains the dominant language of the ISA sessions and its publications and many members of the ISA are American, many other members come from Sweden, Norway, Canada, Australia, Germany, Britain, India, and Japan. In a sense, the study of international affairs is itself becoming globalized. And while previously it was mainly political scientists and economists who came to ISA's annual meetings—*as if* it took only political science and economics to make sense of national security, international trade, war, peacemaking, migration, diplomacy, oil, and sneakers—today when the ISA gathers, the conference rooms, hotel corridors, and coffee shops are full of historians, sociologists, and anthropologists, too.

Simultaneously, and maybe as a result, the ISA—this transnational intellectual group whose members see themselves as the crafters of political skills and knowledge—has become far less masculinized. That is, there are more women taking part in its annual sessions and in running the organization, *and* it is less acceptable for men, who remain the majority of the organization's members, to dismiss the idea of women as experts and to devalue the study of women as "beside the point." This demasculinization—achieved slowly and through hard work—has made the association livelier, more open, more intellectually valuable.

The women—and a few men—who achieved this partial (but not yet complete) transformation of the ISA did so through several actions:

44

1. Back in the mid-1980s, these women began to urge other women whose work sheds light on any dimension of international relations to attend ISA's annual meetings.
2. Women faculty urged women graduate students both to attend the ISA and to propose their own paper presentations.
3. These women devised new conference panel topics in order to stretch ISA members' sense of what constitutes "international politics." For example, they created new sessions on "Trafficking in Women," "Gendered Humanitarian Aid," "Masculinity and Weaponry," "Feminist Theories of the State," and "Women in the Revolutions of Nicaragua, Eritrea, and Algeria."
4. They began to develop an alternative "culture" for their ISA panel sessions, making those events more interactive, more encouraging and less competitive, less hierarchical.
5. They created a new section within the association's organization, naming it "Feminist Theory and Gender."
6. A few years later, they launched a new ISA caucus specifically to monitor the relative influence of men and women on the ISA's governing committees.
7. Most recently, the ISA's feminist-informed women and men created a new journal, the *International Feminist Journal of Politics.*

The twenty women and men who launched the *International Feminist Journal of Politics* had long conversations before the launch about how to create a new journal that would be academically and intellectually (these are not necessarily synonymous) serious, respected, and valued, while at the same time did not reproduce some of the traits they had all come to see as hallmarks of masculinized academic-journal-editing practice—a practice that narrows and dampens the knowledge sharing required to do serious gender research on international relations. Here are a few things they together decided would be necessary if the *International Feminist Journal of Politics* were to achieve both of these ambitious goals.

First, the journal headquarters would always have to be located *outside* the United States. This decision came out of a recognition that in today's globalized academic world, American universities, publishers, and scholars play a disproportionate role due to the dominance of English, the size of the country, the number of its universities and colleges, the predominance of U.S. foreign policy actions throughout most regions of the world, and the economic power of U.S.-based media. Thus, while American academics serve as members of the editorial advisory board, contribute articles, and occasionally serve as one of the trio of chief editors, the headquarters was located first in Australia and then in Britain, and is now located in Canada.

Second, the journal's founding group decided that there would be three chief editors, rotating every three years, and that these editors would always come from three different geographic regions. Third, the group decided that "blind" reviewers would give suggestions and criticisms of all submitted articles in a spirit of collegial helpfulness. The founders also wanted submissions from young scholars to be encouraged. Fourth, the founders decided that the journal would welcome potential articles from any academic field that sheds light on the ways in which international relations becomes gendered. The journal would "toss overboard" the common assumption that scholars trained in political science are the only ones who can show us how the international system works—and why.

The multinational group of founders made another important decision: this journal would not shy away from a feminist identity. "Feminist" would be printed in bold letters as part of the new journal's title. On the other hand, the journal would not adopt a static, a parochial, or a single definition of "feminist," because the founders all had learned how place-, time-, and culture-specific feminist analyses can be.

Finally, during these lively discussions in the mid-1990s— discussions that produced what they hoped would become a new kind of forum for the serious investigation of international politics—the journal's founders decided that every issue would contain a featured section called "Conversations," a place where alternative forms of serious intellectual discussion of "international politics" could appear—interviews, conference reports, even film reviews. That is, they recognized that globalizing politics occurs in many arenas, not just inside governments or within international agencies.

Integral to all of these intellectual endeavors by feminist scholars has been challenging the long-established, conventional concept of—and explanations for—"national security." The hunch has been that if we think outside the "state security box," if we take seriously the lives of women—their understandings of security—as well as the on-the-ground workings of masculinity and femininity, we will be able to produce more meaningful and more reliable analyses of "security"—personal, national, and global (Hansen and Olsson 2004).

By employing a feminist curiosity—that is, by asking (and seeking to answer) hard questions about diverse women's relationships to men, to the nation, to the state, and to other women, as well as questions about how men's relationships to diverse notions of masculinity affect women's lives and the operations of politics—scholars and teachers are seeking to get a more realistic and less militarized understanding of what "security" means now and what it could potentially mean in the future. These scholars are discovering that ideas (and policies) about masculinity and about femininity are frequently the consequence of "national security" doctrines—for example, that the more militarized the criteria adopted for national security, the more it is only men who are presumed to be those most trusted to handle foreign policymaking, and that anyone imagined to be "feminine" is often deemed unsuited for the "hard" thinking involved in this realm called national security.

On the other hand, ideas about masculinity and femininity might be the *cause* of national security choices. That is, as we saw in the case of globalized sneaker politics, when we use a feminist curiosity we shine a search light not just on impacts but also on causality.

Take the ongoing investigations into why the U.S. government under several presidents pursued military solutions to political problems in the small Southeast Asian country of Vietnam so persistently. In the summer of 2004, Daniel Ellsberg was still puzzling about this. Daniel Ellsberg, as a young man in 1971 was working under contract for the U.S. Defense Department. He became a hero to many and a traitor in the eyes of some when he secretly photocopied hundreds of pages of an in-house government report analyzing the policy failures of the United States in waging its war in Vietnam. President Richard Nixon failed in his attempts to convince the Supreme Court that national security necessity made it legal to stop the public release of the damning report. The report, read by millions of Americans and people around the world after it was published in the *New York Times* and the *Washington Post*, became known as the *Pentagon Papers*. In 2004, more than three decades later, Daniel Ellsberg was still wondering why Nixon's predecessor, Lyndon B. Johnson, so stubbornly persisted in waging a war that even his closest advisors were telling him was unwinnable and was growing deeply unpopular among many Americans.

Ellsberg, speaking to a group of peace-activist military veterans in July 2004, wondered out loud what motivated President Johnson's refusal to back down from his failing war-waging policy. After years of thinking about this question and weighing all the alternative answers, Ellsberg told his audience that he had come to the conclusion that it was not President Johnson's anticommunist ideology and not his famous electoral calculations. Rather, Ellsberg had concluded, it was President Johnson's fear of being thought of as "unmanly." It was his anxiety fueled by imagining that if he backed away from a military engagement, he would open himself to charges of being, in American slang, a "wimp"—of not having the masculine credentials to see a country through a war, even a failed and unpopular war.

The jury is still out regarding why Presidents Lyndon Johnson and Richard Nixon were so persistent in their commitment to a U.S. military engagement in Vietnam, in which over 50,000 U.S. soldiers and thousands more Vietnamese—and Cambodian and Laotian—soldiers and civilians died. But it is worth taking seriously Daniel Ellsberg's carefully considered argument. Which of the many militarized foreign policy decisions made by any senior government official in any country is affected even in part by their personal worries about not appearing "feminine"?

Or let's look at the more recent experiences of the international civilian weapons inspectors sent to Iraq by the United Nations in 2002. This was a highly masculinized team—that is, it was widely believed within the United Nations and the UN Security Council that only men had the sorts of attitudes and technical expertise appropriate to conduct this politically loaded international scientific weapons inspection. Nonetheless, despite its conformity to the conventions of masculinized international security affairs, the team, headed by Swedish diplomat Hans Blix, had its findings repeatedly challenged by the Bush administration in the months of tense UN debates leading up to the eventual U.S. preemptive military invasion of Iraq in March 2003.

Feminist scholar Carol Cohn wondered why. She decided to dig more deeply into this international politics of weapons inspection and its failure of credibility at such a critical moment in the evolving post–Cold War global politics of security. After all, the United Nations was created in 1945 to help roll back global militarization, to make wars less likely. Why had it seemingly failed in March 2003?

Cohn and her coresearchers, Felicity Hill and Sara Ruddick, were invited in 2005 to Stockholm to present their analysis of the international politics of weapons inspections to the members of the prestigious Weapons of Mass Destruction Commission (WMDC). The audience, composed of former ambassadors, senior UN officials, and former secretaries and ministers of defense, also included Hans Blix himself. Most of the people there in the hall that day were quite new to feminist analysis (Cohn 2005).

Here is what Cohn, Ruddick, and Hill reported to their rather skeptical Stockholm listeners. The internationally heated debate during 2002 and early 2003 was over whether the government of President Saddam Hussein was developing weapons of mass destruction, as President George W. Bush and his advisors were contending—and which contentions were being made the basis for developing elaborate plans for a U.S.-led military invasion of Iraq to topple the Saddam Hussein regime. The Hans Blix team reported back to the UN Security Council that its months of on-site inspections had turned up no evidence that the Iraqi government had an active program of developing weapons of mass destruction. The Bush administration, speaking to its own American legislators and citizens, as well as to its comembers of the UN Security Council, dismissed the Blix team's findings as not credible, thus justifying its own continued buildup for a military invasion and its pressure on the governments of Britain, Australia, Spain, the Ukraine, Japan, Italy, and Honduras to commit their own troops to a U.S.-led military invasion. Credibility turned out to be the principal currency in what had become a high-stakes and potentially deadly global game.

Carol Cohn and her coinvestigators shined a feminist curiosity light on political credibility. What creates it? What undermines it? In whose eyes? They discovered that the Bush administration repeatedly cast doubt on the credibility of mere diplomats. The powerful strand of American political culture that values manly shows of overt strength over allegedly "softer" or more feminized demonstrations of patient, careful negotiations had become even more dominant in the wake of the attacks of September 11, 2001. Thus, in various public settings, the Bush administration portrayed the civilian UN inspectors as somehow less trustworthy and less credible because they were following a course of action that was less committed to a demonstration of physical force. The drama of the months leading up to the U.S. military invasion of Iraq was a contest between masculinities.

The largely male audience in Stockholm listening to Cohn, Hill, and Ruddick's analysis were not immediately convinced. Most of the audience had never thought it necessary to develop the skills with which to conduct a feminist analysis of international or national security. Yet when Carol Cohn met one of the prominent members of the WMDC several months later, he went out of his way to tell her that he had continued to think about her talk and about the role that competing ideas about masculinity had played in the political contest between the UN weapons inspectors and the Bush administration. And, he admitted, he'd begun to think for the first time that ideas about, and demonstrations of, masculinity may have been decisive in the final outcome.

When it came to writing their two hundred-page annual report, members of the WMDC inserted just one short paragraph indicating that gendered analysis was starting to make an impact on their collective thinking:

> Women have rightly observed that armament policies and the use of armed force have often been influenced by the misguided ideas about masculinity and strength. An understanding of and emancipation from this traditional perspective might help to remove some of the hurdles on the road to disarmament and non-proliferation. (Weapons of Mass Destruction Commission 2006, 160)

A postscript: According to one WMDC commissioner, this brief nod to gendered analysis did not get inserted by the commission into its report because of a broad consensus among the members that gender matters. Rather, this commissioner confidentially recalled, a reference to the influence of the politics of masculinity on global nuclear, chemical, and biological weapons proliferation went into the report only at the insistence of one of the few women on the commission, an experienced international civil servant. Had she not been in the room, the insights offered by Cohn, Hill, and Ruddick might never have seen the light of day.

This experience suggests that a brief flash of gendered understanding on the parts of men and women whose professional careers have depended on not acknowledging the impacts of femininity and masculinity will not be sustained—for instance, in ongoing international diplomatic political discussions with the governments of Iran and North Korea—if there aren't persistent institutional encouragements and affirmations to support that initial flash of understanding. Ideas matter. But ideas need to be nurtured by formal and informal social (including institutional) dynamics. One of the reasons that ungendered explanations of militarization are so persistent is that they are the explanations that, when offered at a closed meeting or over supper or in a public debate, are treated as "rational," "serious," and "sophisticated."

Asking feminist questions in the study of national and global security, thus, includes asking the following questions about masculinity:

- Who holds what views of manliness?
- Who wields those ideas in political life?
- What are the consequences of those views and ideas?

Investigating all three questions also requires keeping a close eye on femininity: who fears it, why, and with what results.

The answers in any particular circumstance aren't preordained. Taking the questions seriously and crafting strategies to pursue them carefully will make us smarter.

As these two cases suggest, militarization of global affairs is likely to be propelled forward by *masculinization*. Yes, another "ization" to monitor. Like globalization and militarization, masculinization should be investigated as a step-by-step process. So, to make sense of a process—globalization, militarization, masculinization—we again need to think like a historian, not a photographer.

Masculinization, as we have seen, often is fueled by key players' anxieties and fears of *feminization*. Any person or group of people who think that if they are perceived to be "feminine" they will lose political influence, credibility, or respect, are likely to take steps to avoid being perceived that way: they will stay quiet about their genuine reservations; they might speak publicly about the values of strength and decisive threatening action; they will make clear that they personally are always ready to wield military might; they might even cast doubt on the manliness of those who are criticizing military solutions (diplomats, pacifists, "the French").

Masculinization, consequently, can be reliably studied only if observers keep a close eye on the processes of feminization. Globalization can be propelled by efforts at each. The globalized sneaker industry (and computer, garment, toy, and food processing industries) has been made more profitable by using ideas about alleged feminine dexterity and marriage and family duties. Simultaneously, the globalization of militaristic solutions has been furthered by the awarding of the politically valuable label "manly" to those who define security in militarized terms. Indian feminists, for instance, have been especially critical of their own government officials for heralding India's nuclear weapons tests as proof of their own Indian manliness (Oza 2006). When, in 2006, both the U.S. president and Congress affirmed the Indian government's violation of nuclear nonproliferation—even though the United States is one of the signatories of the international treaty to limit nuclear proliferation—the Indian officials' politics of masculinity seemed to be reaping global rewards.

Masculinization can proceed part way and then be resisted and stalled. Thus, one needs to monitor—and explain—every step along the way. This means that we need to use our feminist curiosity to explain how and why any state's notion of "national security" has become militarized or masculinized to a large degree or only to a lesser degree. But we won't uncover the answers if we ignore or trivialize the lives of women.

For example, women activists in both Afghanistan and Iraq who have been monitoring the international politics of rebuilding their badly damaged countries have noted how masculinized the new systems of power are. These women explain that, despite quotas for women in the new national legislatures being put in place by the U.S. government in post-invasion Iraq and by the United States together with UN agencies in post-invasion Afghanistan, the security forces (police, military, and special armed protection forces) are both overwhelmingly male and infused with masculinized organizational cultures. Simultaneously, scores of nongovernmental militias controlled in Iraq by civilian political parties and in Afghanistan by regional power brokers (sometimes called "warlords") continue not only to exist but to wield power in provinces and neighborhoods. They too are both overwhelmingly male and infused with presumptions about masculine privilege and about manliness expressed through the wielding of violence (Filkins 2006). With such thoroughly masculinized and militarized forces holding sway over the political life of both Iraq and Afghanistan, what meaningful chance do politically engaged civilian women (who of course are themselves diverse) have to have their opinions translated into public policies?

Insofar as answering this important question is kept off the agenda of most of the international actors operating in Iraq or Afghanistan, masculinized militarization is being globalized.

We should add a new concept to our analytical (explanatory) toolbox only if we believe it will sharpen our understanding of reality. If any proposed new (or old) concept actually blurs or distorts our understanding of reality, then we should put it back on the shelf, maybe even toss it out. I find it helpful to judge the usefulness of any concept in the same way that I judge a flashlight. Someone hands you a flashlight and you say, "I wonder if it is a good flashlight." So you go into a darkened room, you turn it on, and you judge if corners of the room previously in the shadows now become easier to see than before. If you find that this particular flashlight distorts the shapes in the room or if the beam is too weak and you still trip over objects on the floor, then you return that flashlight with a polite "thank you."

Let's be very practical about adding or adopting any concept. We should never use a concept (or impose it on our readers or our fellow students) just because it's rather pleasing aesthetically—that is, merely because we like the way we sound when we use it—or because people with influence use it.

Here I'm imagining "masculinization," "feminization," "militarization," and "globalization" as four conceptual flashlights. By offering them to you, I'm hoping to provide tools for shining a brighter, wider, more realistic light on the local and international political dynamics of "national security." You will have to try out these offered flashlights in the rooms you are exploring, and then you can come to your own judgment as to their practical value.

When I first started trying to make sense of security policy, I thought that I needed just two concepts in my analytical toolbox: "militarism" and "the military." The first—"militarism"—was a package of distinct but interdependent values and beliefs about how the world "works" and how the world ought to work. The second concept—"the military"—was meant to distinguish a particular sort of institution. According to this concept, a military was distinct from a family, a baseball team, a political party, a corporation, even from a police force. I thought that, equipped with these two concepts, I could adequately shed an explanatory light on national and international security politics.

I was wrong. What I slowly began to realize was that relying on the concepts of "militarism" and "militaries" would not enable me to explain how the politics of what was defined as "national," and what was defined as "security" might change from one decade to another. In other words, with only the flashlights of "militarism" and "military" in my toolbox, I could see parts of the room but not enough of it to build a satisfactory explanation for how the world actually works. I found that I could not understand how in any given society—Nigeria, Sudan, Cambodia, Egypt, Israel, the United States, Argentina—militarism, that package of beliefs and values, had come to gain a foothold: how could this particular package of ideas have been weak in the past yet later become so strong that most elites and many ordinary citizens imagined that "national security" and militarism were synonymous?

"Militarism" was still a useful concept, but not useful enough. It turned out to be too static. I could measure popular and elite ideas against it, but I could not explain how and why changes in either popular or elite presumptions had been transformed over a year, a decade, or a generation. I found that I wanted to explain the politics of national security—to expose its causes. Why did that person—or that political party or that agency—in an effort to achieve national security, become more dependent on militaristic strategies? Why then? Why not earlier? Why not later?

Adopting militarization as a "flashlight," I also became curious about the broad *politics* of things most of my political science colleagues dismissed back then as not really "political": the politics of marriage, of fear, of workplace morale, of identity. And I then discovered that I couldn't adequately explore any of these political concepts unless I took women seriously.

At this point in my development, I started to pay close attention to the smart research of other feminists on schemes by war planners, military juntas, and defense administrators to control women—efforts to control women's fears, women's ambitions, women's sense of belonging, women's sexuality, and women's labor. Works by feminist historians investigating World Wars I and II began to crowd out the more conventional political science books on my shelves.

I started to attend panel sessions at conferences on popular culture and on cross-cultural constructions of femininity. I changed the sort of assignments I gave students in my seminars. Now I urged each student to do an in-depth interview with any woman—of any age, any class, any nationality—to see if that woman had ever been dependent on, influenced by, or controlled by a military. What these thoughtful, curious students revealed as they each tried to make sense of the life of just one woman, was that militarization was an often subtle, nuanced, even confusing, sometimes sporadic, often contested process.

Military wives. These women seem so far away from the pinnacles of state power. Nevertheless, I have been continually surprised to find it as revealing (and mind expanding) to pay close attention to military wives—to those women who are married to the state's soldiers and possess little political influence—as to pay attention to, for example, the better-known women heads of government Indira Gandhi of India, Margaret Thatcher of Britain, Gro Brundtland of Norway, Benazir Bhutto of Pakistan, or Helen Clark of New Zealand (all of whom, nonetheless, are diverse in their political stances on militarization).

Here is what I learned by taking seriously the lives of military wives: masculinized government officials in many countries—for instance, the United States, Canada, Israel, Japan, Russia, Iran, and Britain—have spent a lot of time and energy trying to socialize and control those women who have married their state's soldiers. Many women have found real satisfaction and rewards in trying to live up to the government's—and their husband's—expectations. These women have been able to see themselves as genuine patriots for doing all that the government needs them to do:

- moving frequently
- sacrificing their own career aspirations
- volunteering for unpaid work to keep a military base community together
- enduring the loneliness of single motherhood when their soldier-husbands are deployed far away
- staying publicly cheerful while privately coping with the possible bouts of anger and depression that their husbands may experience after stints in tense combat zones
- not asking too many questions about the possible sexual liaisons their husbands might have engaged in when away from home
- staying quiet in their grief if their husbands are killed while deployed

Some women gain in social and economic status by marrying a soldier, especially if he earns promotions up through the ranks of the military's officer corps. As a bonus, some women married to soldiers like the close community they experience on a military base, and they take pride in their children's capacity to adapt to new environments (Alva 2006).

On the other hand, some women married to soldiers have refused to conform to the official expectations of how the proper military wife should behave—for instance, by encouraging their husbands not to reenlist, by speaking out about domestic violence perpetrated by soldier-husbands and soldier-boyfriends against their wives and girlfriends, by criticizing the policies that deprive senior officers' wives of military health care and housing benefits when their husbands file for divorce, despite the years of service many of these women have contributed to the community life on military bases, or (hardest of all) by speaking out as the civilians that they in fact are about their government's foreign policy. When military wives take any of these unusual steps, officials get nervous. They try to brush domestic violence inside military families under the rug. They try to provide benefits to war widows. They publicly portray the entire military as a "family." They enlist other military wives as the chief socializers of women who have recently married soldiers. Despite all this effort, however, in many policymaking settings, military officials commonly may act as though military wives are a bother, a distraction from the military's primary mission (Harrison and Laliberte 1994; Harrison 2002; Lutz 2001; Houppert 2005; Eran-Jona 2005; Zahedi 2006; Alvarez 2006).

The efforts that officials of many countries devote to controlling military wives are carried out with minimal fanfare. A lot of the socializing is done by other military wives, who out of friendship and the desire to keep the military community harmonious, instruct women newly married to soldiers on how to behave. Still, there are a lot of decisions made by officials to sustain the expected behavior and attitude among women married to soldiers. Most of these decisions about military wives (a majority of whom are civilians, formally outside the military) are made far down the bureaucratic ladder, where nobody notices. Until recently, almost no scholars invested their research energies into understanding military wives. Rarely did any teacher of global affairs or international politics dedicate a week of a semester's syllabus to delving into the lives of military wives. Certainly the influential Japanese newspaper the *Asahi Shimbun*, CNN, and Reuters have only occasionally assigned reporters to cover the politics of military wives.

Despite this academic and media inattention, military wives learning to admire a militarized form of masculinity in their husbands and military wives complying with the government's own models of militarized marriage, I discovered, were indeed integral to those governments' preferred "national security" doctrines.

When we try to explain any government official's masculinized "national security" policies, we are tempted to imagine that these women married to soldiers are a trivial concern. "Trivial" is worth pausing to think about. We tend to pay little attention to anything

57

that can be dismissed as trivial. Thus, one of the assumptions I had to overcome when I began, cautiously, to pay attention to military wives was that maybe I was wasting my time: maybe military wives were merely "trivial." Behind that dismissive attitude were the beliefs that women married to soldiers scarcely wielded influence with their own husbands and that women married to soldiers had no impact on ideas about technology or enemies or allies or violence. Moreover, I had to take a close look at my previous trivializing assumption that women married to soldiers are of no concern to state planners because they are just women "doing what comes naturally." For anything that happens naturally—a woman going along with whatever career choices her husband made and with the daily consequences of her husband's career choice—seems unworthy of serious investigation.

Yet no one is born an obedient, flexible, loyal, patriotic woman, a woman who loves swinging back and forth between living sometimes like a grateful dependent and other times like a resourceful single parent. A woman has to be persuaded, and sometimes is pressured, to become—and stay—a "model military wife." The design and implementation of those persuasion and pressure techniques has been an unexamined part of governments' "national security" operations.

That is, if too many women married to soldiers rebel—divorce their soldier-husbands or refuse to revert to grateful dependency after having spent months crafting the skills of independent lone parenthood, or start talking to journalists of their doubts about the government's foreign policies—many officials see those women not simply as falling short of a feminized militarized marital ideal but as threats to national security. Such women come to be seen by commanders (and sometimes other more progovernment military wives) as "problem wives," insofar as their actions might weaken the morale of soldier-husbands or might weaken popular resolve to accept the costs of the government's policies. Precisely because it is so popularly imagined that military wives are "naturally" patriotic and that their patriotism will take the form of accepting what their government's officials need from both them and their husbands, when military wives do speak out critically, their opinions attract attention—and often harsh criticism.

Researcher Monica Henry heard women married to American soldiers detail their fears about speaking out when she interviewed them during the Iraq war. Many military wives told Henry that they supported the U.S. government's invasion and occupation of Iraq, explaining to her that their trust in the president, their support of the president's foreign policy in Iraq, and their loyalty to their husbands deployed to Iraq were all of a single piece. Yet those military wives who had become critical of the war said it was very risky to voice their opinions out loud: if a military wife spoke out, military commanders could hear of it and perhaps hinder her husband's career; the military wife herself might be ostracized by other military wives, on whose support she may depend during her husband's months overseas; an outspoken military wife might find her on-base job jeopardized. As one longtime military wife, who used the Internet pseudonym "Love My Tanker," told Henry, "Although it doesn't say this anywhere in any regulations, etc., if I am a problem wife, the chain of command will know about it . . . Everything I do or do not do, say or do not say, could have an impact on my husband . . . The military is actually a small place" (Henry 2006, 46).

Suddenly the topic of women married to soldiers no longer looks "trivial."

My own gradual discovery has been that the conventional menu of "serious" topics for a student of national security is much too short. By prioritizing so few topics in undergraduate and graduate school curricula, professional journals, and think-tank research projects, many conventional national security intellectuals have shrunk their own curiosities. By dismissing as irrelevant, for instance, the dynamics of competitive masculinities and government efforts to control military wives, many national security specialists simultaneously have militarized *and* masculinized their own academic field of inquiry.

This trivializing tendency, in turn, has made it harder to see the intellectual presumptions of those engaged in the study of national and international security. It is not surprising, then, that it has been "outsiders"—researchers and teachers using a feminist curiosity— who have pushed open creaking doors, raised dusty windows, and shone new light into dimly lit rooms, and who have thereby provided a fresh alternative to the older masculinized and militarized menu of topics and questions to delve into as we seek a clearer understanding of "national security" politics.

One of the most powerful ideas that has made the militarization of national security seem "natural" (i.e., not worth questioning) is the notion that there is an allegedly "natural" relationship between the protected and the protector. It takes a feminist curiosity and gender-analysis skills to lift up these two heavy rocks of national security studies and policymaking so we can critically scrutinize what ideas lie under both of them. Conventional ideas about this protected-protector relationship appear to perpetuate the political assumption that in any community some people are naturally the protectors while others are naturally the protected.

Going against the grain of this conventional wisdom, historians studying marriage and girls' education, sociologists examining family law, activists trying to stop domestic violence, women's studies researchers investigating military conscription, and feminist labor activists together have given us an alternative understanding of the politics of the protector and protected and have revealed just how pervasive this gendered protector-protected system has become. They also have exposed the extent to which this widespread assumption can distort power relations: it is much easier to claim the authority to speak for others if one can claim to be The Protector; it is much easier to be silenced and to accept that silencing if one absorbs the self-identity of The Protected.

We have only begun to apply this critical analysis of socially constructed protection to the field of "national security." In applying this feminist knowledge to national security politics, we are rejecting the belief that our knowledge about the history of marriage, of child custody, of divorce, and of domestic violence is relevant "only" to the local arenas of public affairs. Instead, we are showing that a feminist historian of marriage (or of education or of violence against women) is indeed exactly the right "expert" to place on a panel to discuss nuclear weapons proliferation. We are demonstrating that useful, eye-opening discussions of foreign policy and military influences will result from exactly this sort of intellectual conversation.

An allegedly "natural" protector is the person who has not just the physical strength or the collective physical resources to wield definitive power but who—allegedly—is most capable of thinking in a certain way: more "strategically," more "rationally." The protectors are those who can see beyond the minutiae of daily life—those who have the ability to see the Big Picture. In any patriarchal society, the protectors are deemed to be the natural controllers of the protected not merely because they are stronger than the protected but because they are (allegedly) smarter. They can act "for their own good." The masculinization of national security studies and of national security policymaking therefore flows directly out of the patriarchal belief that one has to be "manly" in order to be rational enough to be responsible for the security of "women and children."

For the protectors to wield this public superiority, there must be a certain constructed "protected." The protected is the person who is not at ease in the public sphere. The protected's natural habitat is the domestic sphere—that is, the sphere of life where caring matters more than strategizing. Consequently, the protected is feminized insofar as the protected needs somebody who can think strategically and act in her (the protected's) best interests. This masculinization of the protector and its necessary feminization of the protected has far-reaching implications. First, such a process of masculinization justifies state secrecy. The most "manly" state policymakers and their academic advisers are the only ones rational enough to keep secrets. Less manly (i.e., less rational, less strategically "tough-minded") men—most (not all) elected legislators, most civil servants working in the more feminized departments of the state (e.g., health, culture, environment), most (not all) male journalists—and virtually all women can be excluded from the "top secret" inner circles of national security.

Today it is more urgent than ever to be curious about this relationship between the alleged protectors and the alleged protected. Those who now claim to be the nation's protectors have a stake in portraying the world as (and turning the world into) a "dangerous place." If we turn our feminist "flashlights" to the processes of making and justifying national security "policies," I think we will find that state elites—with the help of media editors, technical experts, and husbands—invest a lot of effort in keeping afloat this artificial, unequal relationship between the protectors and protected. But we will also discover that this politically charged relationship is frequently challenged, even if those challenges are ignored by the patriarchal media. For instance, when Tokyo women take part in the Friday evening Women in Black peace vigils in busy, neon-lit Shinjuku and hold up signs that declare "Not in Our Name!" they are deliberately disrupting the patriarchal masculinized protector–feminized protected dichotomy on which most "national security" systems are built.

Women in many countries who have begun to make "Not in Our Name!" their own political declaration are proclaiming that they are not merely the feminized protected. They are *citizens*.

PAYING CLOSE ATTENTION TO WOMEN *INSIDE* MILITARIES

The woman soldier. By the early years of the twenty-first century, the woman soldier seemed to have become a globalized icon of the "modern woman": she was breaking into a traditionally masculin- ized domain, she was being deployed far from home, she was dis- playing her physical strength, she was handling high-tech weaponry, and she was wielding authority and proving that she could be the protector, not simply the protected—she too could "die for her country." To some, the woman soldier was thereby showing that a woman could be a "first-class citizen" in her own country and a "peacekeeper" around the world.

The woman soldier was appearing everywhere. She was smiling out from a Japanese Self-Defense Forces recruiting advertisement; she was looking boldly right at you from the Swedish military's web- site; she was marching in Vietnam's patriotic veterans' parades; she was singing the national anthem at an American sporting event.

There seemed to be a halo of modernity around this woman sol- dier. And we have learned that pursuit of modernity is one of the incentives that governments and individuals find appealing for join- ing the process of globalization. For some people, no military could claim to be a genuinely "modern military" unless it allowed at least some women to join its ranks. In the late 1990s, Italy was the last of all the NATO countries to permit women to enlist. The all-male military seemed to be going the way of the all-male college. Modernity, that pot of gold at the end of the global rainbow, demanded that at least some women be permitted access to soldiering.

This iconic image of the woman soldier was reminiscent of an earlier globalized image of the modern woman. She was popularly called—and often proudly called herself—the "New Woman." During the 1910s and 1920s, she too popped up all over the world. In cities such as Istanbul, Seoul, Shanghai, Tokyo, Paris, Chicago, Toronto, and London, she was the young woman who left her small town and migrated to the city. As a New Woman, she thrived on the lively bustle and seeming freedom of the big city. She wanted to experience independence, earning her own wages in an office job and living with women friends in a boarding house or rented apartment away from the confines of family supervision. The New Woman dressed in the newly relaxed fashions and read books and slick magazines written for her and about her. She resisted marriage until it could be on her own terms. In many places she was exercising her newly won right to vote; in some places she was joining with other women to create public campaigns to open up new opportunities for women (Ito and Morimoto 2004; Ito 2006; Kwon 2000).

Some of these New Women were, just as some of the contemporary women soldiers are, feminists; that is, they deliberately analyzed, critiqued, and collectively challenged the power systems that operate daily to keep women socially confined, physically constrained, economically dependent, and politically sidelined. Many other women who earlier aspired to become a New Woman or who today enlist in the military, however, eschew feminism. These women, though adventurous, have been afraid that if they are seen by their colleagues or the general public as "feminists," they will have a harder time achieving their own unconventional personal goals.

The contemporary woman soldier and the earlier New Woman each was the object of popular hope and admiration. But, not surprisingly, each was—and still is—the target of intense debate and even scorn, since both the woman soldier and the New Woman— even if they did not embrace the label "feminist"—undermined assumptions about biology, respectability, and femininity, and thereby raised new discomforting questions about the roles and privileges of men.

The New Woman was a globalizing phenomenon. Women in Seoul traveled to Tokyo to meet and study with those Japanese women writers and artists whose liberated lives they admired. Women in China and Japan translated and put on productions of Norwegian playwright Henrik Ibsen's controversial play *A Doll's House*, which portrays one woman's rebellion against her claustrophobic middle-class marriage.

So too today women in militaries often—not always—develop a global awareness and create their own international networks. They are keen to find out what is going on in the lives of women soldiers in other countries. They meet and compare notes when they are deployed on joint peacekeeping operations, when they travel abroad for special training courses, or when they gather for conferences sponsored by various advocacy groups to discuss the continuing barriers women soldiers face when seeking promotions or simply respect: "Are you allowed to serve in combat roles?" "Do your superiors ignore women's complaints of sexual harassment?" "How have you managed to get your veterans' hospitals to offer services that address women's reproductive health issues?" (Manning 2006).

For all their intriguing similarities, however, the New Woman of the 1910s and 1920s and today's woman soldier are marked by a major difference. The New Woman was typically the object of contempt and even fear (she was tearing apart the nation, she was upsetting the "social order"). By stark contrast, women in state militaries—if they stay in the roles the state assigns them—are there because government strategists think they will enhance "national security": (a) they will make up for the loss of middle-class men caused by the repeal of male conscription laws ("the draft"), (b) they will compensate for a decline in the country's birthrate (because many women are having fewer babies than they did a generation ago), (c) they will allow the government not to recruit "too many" men from those ethnic and racial groups the government's elite doesn't respect or trust, (d) they will bring with them higher levels of formal education than many of the country's young men achieve, and of course, (e) they will help make the government's military look "modern" in the eyes of many of its own citizens and observers abroad. As was true of the earlier New Women, these women in to-day's militaries provoke mixed responses, both admiration and anxiety. Each group of women can benefit their countries, many observers seem to imply, only if their energies and talents can be controlled.

That "if" matters: *if* women in the military stay in the actual and the symbolic roles their male superiors assign them. But that condition can be tough to sustain when women in any military start making alliances with supportive civilian legislators or when the military is stretched thin and needs to open up loopholes to make maximum use of all personnel—male and female, young and old, gay and straight, racially privileged and racially marginalized. Thus, in connection with the current U.S. wars in Afghanistan and Iraq, observers noted that despite denials by senior officials that American women were in "combat"—that hallowed role reserved for "manly" men—in practice, women soldiers deployed to both Iraq and Afghanistan were routinely assigned to combat operations (Solaro 2006).

What can we learn, then, from taking women soldiers in the military seriously? If they have become, for many people, a widespread symbol of the "modern military," are they helping to globalize militarization?

So far in these chapters, we have explored four themes. First, we have tried to discover what it means to develop a *feminist* curiosity. Second, we have moved beyond merely describing the impacts of militarization on women to reveal how ideas about women and about femininity often are *causes* of certain globalizing political trends. Third and fourth, to help us make sense of globalization, we have weighed the analytical uses of two concepts: *masculinization* and *militarization*.

Now I would like to propose a fifth theme and a new conceptual "flashlight" to help us illuminate this complex world—*patriarchy*.

Patriarchy is a concept that allows us to shine a bright light on a particular way of organizing relationships. In other words, patriarchy sums up—allows us to see—a distinctive social structure. And, like capitalism, feudalism, or democracy, patriarchy is a structure based on (i.e., dependent on the continued acceptance of) a particular set of beliefs (about how and why humans and nature behave)

and values (the "best," "most moral," "most rational" ways for humans and nature to operate).

Any patriarchal group or society is based on several fundamental
beliefs:

- Women and men are intrinsically and unalterably different
  from one another.
- These presumably natural differences explain why women and
  men (rightly) play distinctly different roles in society.
- Men are natural—and superior—income earners, explorers,
  inventors, corporate executives, security strategists, public authorities, and heads of households because of their (allegedly)
  distinguishing traits (e.g., greater rationality, greater capacity
  to handle the harsh realities of public life, less natural inclination for child rearing, stronger sex "drive," greater physical
  strength).
- Women's allegedly natural inclinations (e.g., homemaking,
  child rearing, expressing emotion, performing delicate physical tasks) make them valuable in home life and in comforting
  men, who, it is patriarchally believed, shoulder the heavy bur-
  dens of public life. A woman gives this comfort willingly and
  gratefully, believers in patriarchal social orders imagine, because women are so thankful for (and dependent on) men—
  the men who provide them with protection inside their
  families and the men who use their natural masculine skills to
  protect the entire society. Feminized gratitude is crucial to any
  patriarchal system.

While many men and women discuss these patterns and beliefs
among friends, among family members, in the workplace, and during elections, most seem reluctant to assign the entire system a specific name. Most of us prefer to talk about "discrimination," or
maybe "sexism"; that is, we shy away from talking about an entire
structure of societal relationships, and we are more comfortable discussing attitudes. While attitudes—what they are, where they come
from, what their consequences are—do matter, they are not the
whole story. They certainly are not the whole story of either militarized globalization or globalized militarization.

Whenever we find a patriarchal relationship operating, we need to follow up that feminist discovery with a question: what sustains this patriarchy? We also need to ask (ourselves and everyone else): if we ignore the workings of patriarchy here, what will we *inade-quately* (unreliably) explain?

When we ask whether any group, institution, or society is "patri-archal," we will be investigating the extent to which (one needs to be subtle here) the survival and success of this group or institution or society is imagined to be dependent on

- the privileging of masculinity,
- the marginalization of women and anything or anyone deemed "feminine," and
- the perpetuation of those ideas and routine practices (some-times elevated to the status of "traditions") that legitimize and enforce both that kind of privileging and that kind of margin-alization.

For instance, from what you know about the operation of these three main dynamics above, is your college less patriarchal than it was a decade ago? How about your family? Is it in any sense becom-ing more patriarchal—or maybe less—than it was when you were in primary school? Has anyone in your family noticed? And look at your own national legislature. Have the elections of several more women legislators over the last decade made that institution sig-nificantly less patriarchal than it was when there were only two or three women legislators? How can you tell?

To figure out whether any military was, and has remained, a pa-triarchy requires paying close attention to women inside that mili-tary. This is necessary, as we will see, even when women constitute only a small percentage of the total uniformed force.

Why? Because taking women soldiers seriously allows one to see whether the patriarchal inclination to privilege masculinity—to see it as bestowing rationality, public and private authority, leadership potential, intellectual creativity, seriousness, expertise—is lessened when women join men in the ranks. In other words, when women join a previously all-male group, do the patriarchal beliefs and prac-tices that shape that group's culture recede? If they do recede, then maybe the increasing numbers of women soldiers in militaries around the world is contributing to a globalized "depatriarchaliza-tion." True, that's a mouthful, but it would be important.

Despite the diverse intentions of the actual young women who enlist to become soldiers, could more women joining militaries be serving to globalize militarization? That is, even though it might look at first as if women breaking down the barriers of previously male-dominated military institutions is only spreading the norms of equality, maybe in reality, it is a kind of equality that will make mili-taries all the more acceptable around the world, will make militaries appear to be the standard-bearers of enlightened modernity.

Paying attention to women soldiers takes stamina. It entails watching the recruitment strategies and rationales of a government over several decades, while simultaneously listening to women sol-diers from diverse ethnic and racial and socioeconomic back-grounds. For instance, during the 1990s and early 2000s, African American women constituted a surprisingly high percentage of all ac-tive-duty women enlisted in the U.S. Army—that is four times the percentage of African American women among all women in the gen-eral U.S. population (Manning 2005). Since 2000, the percentage of African American women among enlisted women has dropped—from a high of 48 percent in the early 1990s to 38 percent in 2005 (but it is still three times the percentage among all U.S. women). Why did this happen? No one seemed to bother asking because no one had examined the diversity of women soldiers in the first place.

Thus one cannot talk about "American enlisted women" or "South African enlisted women" as if either were a homogeneous so-cial group. Paying attention to women soldiers entails taking seri-ously the diverse experiences of women in the enlisted ranks and officer corps and at the same time, watching the behavior of their male peers and superiors.

"Paying attention" requires listening to silences. When women inside any military (or military academy) do *not* report sexual abuse they have experienced by their male colleagues and superiors—because they decide the military justice system can't be trusted, be-cause they fear being ostracized as "turncoats" by their peers, or because they have seen how other women's careers have been harmed after they have spoken up—*that* is significant. It takes cour-age in any patriarchal institution to raise public objections to masculinized abuse. Thus, for instance, one might pay close attention to the more than one hundred young women in the United States who spoke up during 2005 alone, charging that male military recruiters—from all services—sexually harassed them while in the process of trying to enlist them. Was it somehow easier for these young women to break the silence because they were still civilians and not yet officially in the military? Or were they able to speak out because most of them still lived at home and had older adults, their parents, to give them support when they reported their experiences?

"Paying attention," furthermore, calls for listening to civilians (boyfriends, husbands, mothers, fathers, journalists, elected officials, movie directors, civilian women and men in those countries to which women soldiers are deployed) as they try to weigh the rightness and consequences of women's serving in militaries. For instance, a father who is a military veteran may see his daughter's enlistment as carrying on "the family tradition"—especially if his son does not want to join the military. On the other hand, a civilian boyfriend might start worrying that if he and his soldier-girlfriend get married and she stays in the military, he'll end up like a military wife, acting as a single parent for months while she is deployed overseas.

Yes, this sort of multidimensional "paying attention" is a tall order.

The percentage of women in the military in various countries in 2005 is shown in table 4.1.

We need to treat these percentages—and the percentages in other

Table 4.1   Percentage of women in the military, by country, 2005

Country	% Women	Country	% Women
Australia	13.0	New Zealand	15.0
Britain	8.8	Poland	4.5
Canada	16.3	Russia	10.4
China	6.2	Slovenia	6.0
France	12.8	South Africa	21.7
Germany	5.2	United States	15.0
Netherlands	13.2		

Source: Manning 2005.

countries not so commonly listed, for instance, in Israel (32 percent women—perhaps the highest in the world), Libya, Italy, India, Turkey, Japan, Sweden, and Norway—with caution. They might not be evidence of contemporary "postsexist" enlightenment. First, the percentage of women in any country's military tends to wax and wane over time. It doesn't just continuously increase. For instance, during World War II, the U.S. government deliberately recruited thousands of women—white, African American, Chinese, Japanese, Latina, Native American—to join the Navy's WAVES, the Army's WAC, and the Coast Guard's SPARS, which were branches of the military created by the wartime government especially for women. After the war ended, male officials in the White House, the War Department (then in charge of the Army), the then-Department of the Navy and Congress together chose to demobilize women to the point that they were scarcely visible in the postwar ranks. To make crystal clear their patriarchal point—that a "normal" peacetime military should be a thoroughly masculinized institution—policymakers crafted rules limiting women to a mere 2 percent of the total active-duty force. This was the American military norm throughout the Cold War. The 2 percent limit was kept in place during the Korean and Vietnam wars of the 1950s, 1960s, and early 1970s.

The male leaders of the U.S. Congress, along with their colleagues in the White House and the Defense Department (formerly the War Department and now in charge of all the armed forces, including the newly organized Air Force), didn't decide they needed to lift this ceiling until the early 1970s. What changed? Faced with the increasingly unpopular Vietnam War, American policymakers ended male conscription—what Americans call "the draft"—*without* changing their vision of the U.S. role in the world, which called for a globally deployed military. That is, they ended the male draft, but held on tightly to their presumed need for thousands of new military recruits every year. This obviously posed a dilemma. Their solution: recruit more women. Still, how to do it in a way that would not surrender the military's long-standing attraction as the place where "boys become men"? How to maintain the military's role in sustaining the country's patriarchal social system? It would become a tricky ideological operation.

The Soviet Union's military planners did much the same. They used thousands of women to help wage their fierce World War II battles against the invading German forces. But at the end of the war, they implemented policies allowing the Soviet military to revert to its "natural" masculinized institutional self, dependent on male conscription. Then, in the 1990s, after the breakup of the Soviet Union, the remaining Russian government launched a draining war against rebel forces in the southern province of Chechnya. Service in the Russian military lost its patriotic appeal. Many Russian mothers even began urging their sons to avoid the draft after these women had uncovered the brutal hazing rituals that drove some young conscripts to commit suicide (Sperling 2003). As the war in Chechnya dragged on, disillusionment with military service deepened further still. More young male soldiers went absent without leave (AWOL). It was at this point that Russian military planners began to look favorably on women as recruits (Mathers 2006). In the late 1990s and early 2000s, the government began recruitment campaigns to persuade women to join the military at the same time as many young Russian women were finding it very difficult to get decent jobs in the uncertain Russian civilian employment market.

In neither the United States nor Russia have the male military planners and their legislative colleagues talked about "patriarchy." Those officials and legislators who, after years of deliberately "remasculinizing" their post–World War II militaries, decided to enlist more women volunteers were not motivated chiefly by a desire to liberate women or to lessen masculinized privilege in their country's public life. Instead, they were motivated primarily by their desire to continue wide-ranging military operations at a time when they were losing easy access to young male recruits.

South Africa's story is rather different, at least in its most current chapter. The South African government's efforts to enlist women volunteers began in earnest under the country's racist apartheid regime. As the small white ruling minority began to face stronger resistance from the country's combined black, mixed-race, and Asian majority, the country's political leaders, imbued with patriarchal beliefs derived from a strict brand of Calvinist theology, struggled to sustain a large enough military force to match the new challenge to its authoritarian rule: there weren't enough young white male conscripts to fill the ranks. The apartheid regime thus tried to craft a delicate balancing act. They recruited more black South African male volunteers and at the same time—despite the white male elite's very conservative views about respectable femininity—opened new military roles to women volunteers from all communities, though especially white women.

Then in 1994, when the apartheid regime fell and a new constitutional system was created to ensure nonracist democracy, intense discussions began among South Africans about the appropriate composition of the state's newly reconstructed military. There was agreement that this new postapartheid military should consist wholly of volunteers, not conscripts, and that it should have many more black senior officers. But should it revert to its pre-1980s mostly male composition? South African women's advocates argued that although the just-deposed apartheid elites had recruited large numbers of women into the ranks for the sake of upholding their own racist system, a new democratic military should not simply dismiss women soldiers (Cock 1995). Thus, the fact that today's South African military has one of the world's highest proportions of women in uniform is not the result of a continuation of a recent masculinist and racist political calculation. Rather, it is the product of thoughtful feminist-informed analysis to determine the sorts of relationships between women, the military, and a nascent nonracist political system that would be most likely to ensure a less patriarchal democracy.

Today in dozens of countries there continues an unresolved analytical debate over the magnitude—and direction—of military and societal transformation produced by enlisting more women in the military.

These debates are also going on in other militaries—those of, for example, Norway, India, or Israel. Some Indian defense strategists are arguing that bringing more women into the military will improve the Indian military's peacekeeping operations. While in 2006 only eighteen of India's peacekeeping officers serving on overseas missions are women, that number is due to dramatically increase. One male officer responsible for training Indian army officers for peacekeeping assignments said that women officers were valuable for "their ability to pick up local languages . . . [and for] their knack

73

for integrating their own culture with new ones" (*Hindustan Times* 2006).

Similarly, Norwegians, who like the Indians contribute soldiers to many UN peacekeeping missions, are in the midst of a national conversation about whether more young women should be strongly encouraged to enlist as volunteers in the country's military. Those in favor of raising the proportion of women in the Norwegian military above its currently modest 6 percent believe, like their Indian counterparts, that Norway's role in international peacekeeping would be significantly enhanced if there were more women among its soldiers when they donned their blue UN helmets in efforts to bring calm, trust, and stability to societies torn by conflict. Among these advocates is a Norwegian general. As he explained at a public seminar in Norway in June 2006, from his own experiences on peacekeeping missions in Bosnia and Kosovo, he has concluded that women bring skills to soldiering that are especially pertinent to peacekeeping: they inspire trust among local civilians, especially among local women and children. This belief is grounded in assumptions about femininity, as well as a conviction that these distinctive feminine perspectives and skills would remain undiluted even when women were trained in a largely masculinized force.

By contrast, a longtime Norwegian feminist peace activist addressed the same seminar audience to publicly caution her fellow citizens to stop before they approved the incorporation of significantly more women into the country's military. After all, she and her fellow feminist peace activists warn, although the Norwegian government is among those most dedicated to international peacekeeping and to UN missions, Norway is a member of NATO. And NATO missions are far more militarized. Furthermore, they ask, isn't it as likely that the women brought into the military will absorb a militaristic outlook as it is that their seemingly alternative, less masculinized outlook will shape future operations of the military?

This very same question has been posed by Israeli feminist scholars. While acknowledging that Israel is one of the very few countries in which both women and men are subject to military conscription, these scholars note that women are drafted for shorter terms than men, that most women soldiers are channeled into traditionally feminized military jobs—for instance, secretaries, instructors, nurses, and other administrative positions—and that women are exempted from military service whenever their family responsibilities conflict. In Israeli society, as in most societies, women are seen first and foremost as mothers and daughters, not as architects of the nation's security or as the country's protectors. Most important, it is the male combat soldier who remains the ideal of the true Israeli citizen (Sasson-Levy 2003) Thus, the impressive statistic that 32 percent of the Israeli military are women must be the start, not the end, of a feminist investigation of masculinity, national security, and militarism in Israel—just as such numbers must be the starting points for feminist investigations in other countries.

With that in mind, Israeli feminist investigators have paid close attention to how the Israeli woman soldier is portrayed by the popular Israeli media and by the military establishment itself. Most often, women soldiers are portrayed as conventionally feminine, sexual, and appealing in the eyes of their male colleagues, as if the woman soldier's physical attractiveness played a role in bolstering the morale of male soldiers, who, the images imply, are the ones actually taking the risks and confronting the real dangers in the service of national security (Brownfield-Stein 2006). In any military it is worth monitoring how women soldiers are portrayed in order to chart the ways both the government and ordinary citizens try to balance the competing goals of, on the one hand, enlisting women in the country's protective force and, on the other hand, still maintaining many of their own core patriarchal values and beliefs.

An Israeli feminist scholar who explored the same politics of "having their cake and eating it too" listened closely to those women, a minority of a minority, who have been allowed to hold "nontraditional"—that is, presumably masculinized—jobs in the Israeli Defense Forces (IDF). What she found is that these women have done their best to fit into the IDF's dominant masculinized culture. They have often adopted more masculinized humor, more masculinized modes of walking, and lower voice registers. Most of these women in traditionally masculinized jobs have also tried to deny any experiences of sexual harassment by their male colleagues. For instance, one woman soldier, whom the author calls "Rutti," told of noncommissioned officers in her combat-engineering platoon taunting her with "Rutti is a whore." She never thought of re-

75

porting incidents like this. Instead, Rutti tried to shrug it off, saying, "Obviously, it wasn't fun. It's annoying, but you can't take it too hard. It's a trivial song, nobody notices it, nobody pays attention to it" (Sasson-Levy, 2003). While such a personal interpretation may work as a private survival strategy for a woman isolated in a masculinized institution, letting such misogynistic and harassing practices go unchallenged leaves the existing masculinized military culture firmly in place, perhaps even reaffirmed (Sasson-Levy 2003).

An American feminist researcher who has interviewed college students enrolled in the U.S. military's Reserve Officers' Training Corps (ROTC) would recognize the pattern: she too found that women resorted to personalized strategies rather than challenge the military's dominant culture. The college women in the ROTC that she interviewed tried to balance the conflicting goals of, on the one hand, adopting masculinized posture, lingo, and skills to prove that women can be good soldiers and thus to fit into the dominant group culture and, on the other hand, maintaining sufficiently visible feminine attributes so as not to be written off by their male colleagues as "undatable" (Silva 2006).

The Norwegian feminist peace activist would likely conclude that these Israeli and American research findings confirm her suspicions that merely adding women to the military is not in itself a formula for transforming that military's patriarchal institutional culture or diluting its militarizing influence on the society as a whole.

Discussions about whether women should be enlisted in the military—and, to the extent they are, about which social groups such women should be drawn from, what jobs they should be given, and what proportion of the military should be women—are also taking place today in countries trying to create new governments and new militaries as part of the reconstruction efforts following devastating civil wars. In the postwar (or *one hopes they are* postwar) countries of East Timor, Côte d'Ivoire, Sierra Leone, Bosnia, Croatia, Nepal, Cambodia, Guatemala, Haiti, El Salvador, Somalia, Iraq, and Afghanistan, there are politically fraught conversations taking place—in public and behind closed doors—about who is best recruited into new armed security forces. These discussions involve not just local leaders but an assortment of foreign diplomats, international advisors, overseas trainers, foundation donors, and privately owned contractors receiving government money—all asking difficult questions:

- Who is trustworthy enough to be given a gun?
- Whose exclusion from the new security forces will undermine the fragile peace?
- Whose exclusion won't matter?
- Whose inclusion in the ranks will make the new military trusted by the general citizenry?
- Whose skills are needed?
- Whose immediate needs are best satisfied via the pay and other rewards and benefits that soldiering brings?

Typically, these discussions feature debates about ethnic, regional, racial, class, and political party loyalties—not gender. The unspoken presumption shared by the participants around the table—that is, the local leaders and overseas donors, advisors, and diplomats—frequently is that they are talking about men. Why? Because it is widely believed that it is men's rivalries and unmet needs that will upset the tenuous calm. It is the threats that men pose that must be urgently addressed. And only occasionally is the exclusion of women from the ranks and officer corps of the new military deemed a threat to the fragile postwar peace. Women? Their issues can wait until later. But "later" can be a long time away.

Sometimes, however, the topic of women's inclusion does get on the table, especially if some of the people around the table have broader, less militarized notions of "national security." These people (some perhaps with personal experience in women's grassroots groups) will likely be thinking of dismantling the masculinist culture of the former military, perhaps seeing that masculinist military culture—and not simply past ethnic or partisan loyalties—as at least partly to blame for outbreaks of violence and as sowing the seeds of civilian distrust and alienation. Still, underneath the surface of the discussion will lurk the nagging question: does adding more women to a military have any significant impact at all?

Since the 1980s, some Japanese defense policymakers have adopted a similar mode of thinking. On the one hand, Japan has a constitution that pledges the country both to never again adopt mili-

tary force as a means of resolving problems and to refrain from creating a military with which to wield such force. On the other hand,
today Japan (thanks in part to the strong urging of the U.S. government) actually has a formidable military equipped with the most up-
to-date technology. In practice, the Japanese military, whose formal
name is the Japan Self-Defense Forces (SDF), deploys its soldiers
only on humanitarian missions, and the soldiers never fire their
guns. Yet there is a profound awkwardness that the Japanese must
cope with: the fact that the constitutional antimilitary principle exists side by side with the formidable institutional reality. One way
male policymakers have devised for smoothing out the contradictions that are creating this sense of this political unease is to bring
more Japanese women into the SDF. Women constitute only 4 percent of total SDF personnel, and their roles do not give them much
influence in military decision making. But male policymakers hope
that putting the nonthreatening smiling faces of young SDF women
on the military's recruitment ads and other public relations materials will reassure Japanese supporters of the country's post–World
War II nonaggression principles that the SDF is a friendly, nonviolent institution. For some of the young women soldiers themselves
who enlisted with hopes of avoiding the tokenism they routinely en-
counter in Japanese civilian companies, this superficial public relations ploy generates not pride but disappointment and frustration
(Frühstück 2006).

Now let's take a closer look at the broad debate over what follows
from bringing more women into any military. Look first at the optimists. Optimistic commentators predict that increasing the proportion of women (thus decreasing the proportion of men) in a military
will make that military less patriarchal: the higher the percentage of
women in a military, they believe, the less the traditional privileging
of masculinity will be able to survive. Patriarchal beliefs and ways of
relating simply will prove untenable.

If they are dedicated optimists, they might go further and even
predict that this military will become less militarized. Yes, a less militarized military. What would that look like? Sandra Whitworth, a
Canadian feminist and international politics expert, is very critical
of how militarized the Canadian UN peacekeeping operations have
become. Still, she starts off her thoughtful book about militarized

peacekeeping with a tribute to a seemingly less militarized military: she candidly recalls how glad she was to see Canadian soldiers arrive at her farmhouse in the midst of a brutal ice storm. They were soldiers, but they were also friendly, helpful, nonviolent rescuers (Whitworth 2004).

A less militarized military would be one less imbued with an institutional culture of masculinized violence. It would be a military less committed to a hierarchical, threat-filled worldview; having an "enemy" wouldn't be so central to the military's raison d'être. It would also be a military whose soldiers and their senior officers would take at least as much (or more?) satisfaction in rescuing civilians from the ravages of ice storms, hurricanes, and earthquakes as in rolling into a combat zone in their intimidating armored vehicles. It would be a military in which officers who serve in successful humanitarian operations, not those with combat experience, would have the best chance of being promoted to general or admiral.

According to this optimistic analysis, if, for instance, the proportion of women soldiers rises from just 1 percent of the state's military to 15 percent, masculinization and patriarchy—as well as militarization—will likely be stalled and perhaps even rolled back.

Of course, there is a second possibility. Increasing the percentage of women serving inside the state's military could cause those women to become more militarized. Simultaneously, pessimists predict, the general public's acceptance of women as soldiers will send the roots of militarizing culture down even deeper into the ecology of the entire society. The military with at least 10 percent women in its ranks will no longer look "out of step" with the rest of society. That is, with at least a smattering of women (and featuring those women in recruiting ads, as well as encouraging media coverage of their activities) a military won't look like a bastion of bygone maleness. The military thereby will be harder than ever to distinguish from civilian society. That could make it harder to scrutinize the military's persistent masculinized institutional culture and to raise questions about the military's exemptions from many of the rules and procedures that the civilian public must live by. This more pessimistic analytical forecast is based on the assessment that masculinization, militarization, and patriarchy don't just roll over in the face of change. Each operates within the military as a socializing pressure: the "outsiders" (women) entering the military's realm are likely to adopt as their own the already established—and rewarding—patriarchal beliefs and values.

There is yet a third possibility. Sustaining and challenging patriarchy—these opposing forces might coexist in the same society, or in the same institution. Thus, so too might militarizing and demilitarizing processes. The result would be a surprising mix of pressures and tendencies. An important characteristic of militarized patriarchal states and patriarchal militaries: their policymakers can be confused, contradictory, and ambivalent.

Those men and women who have a stake in perpetuating a patriarchal culture and structure—who see it as good for themselves, good for their families, good for their own society, and even good for the world—are not immune to confusion. For instance, they may want to preserve the dominant masculine culture of their state's military and, *at the same time,* conclude that it is necessary to enlist more women because birthrates are dropping (and so the pool of young men is shrinking), because more male conscripts are going AWOL, or because nervous legislators are responding to the public's disillusionment by voting to end male conscription. Trying to achieve both of these goals can produce confusion and contradictory actions.

The temptation among patriarchal policymakers, however, is to deny confusion—to hide it, to camouflage it under a paint job of convoluted justification. Usually this compels those confused policymakers to spend a lot of energy trying to manipulate definitions of "femininity." In doing this, they will probably look like the South Korean regime of Chung Hee Park, which in the 1960s and 1970s tried to mobilize young women to leave home in order to serve as "cheap labor" in factories, while it simultaneously tried to convince these young women and their parents that "dutiful daughter" was their chief feminine identity.

Any patriarchy survives and thrives only if its leaders and members can perpetuate a widely accepted standard of "proper" femininity. A dominant notion of "proper" femininity is especially potent when it becomes the basis by which women (and girls) judge, or "police," each other. Such daily judging—of girls and women by girls and women—creates divisive hierarchies among women, making it more likely that they will see other girls or women as sources of competition or even as threats to their own sense of well-being. This sort of preoccupation makes it less likely that girls and women will notice how the larger pattern of relationships, rules, and presumptions of patriarchy shapes their own lives, much less that they will join together *as women* to challenge masculinized privilege. That is, when racism, class prejudice, nationalism, patriotism, militarism, and competition for boyfriends and husbands divide women and girls and divert their attention, patriarchy becomes more secure.

Second, if the promoters of a patriarchal system are skillful, they will manage to make "femininity" appear natural—not the product of human decisions. This feat makes their own uses of power harder to see. If they can achieve this, then the entire patriarchal order is likely to take on the status of "natural" and thus not open to fundamental challenge.

Yet as we can see when we pay close attention to women in the military, there are many times when promoters of patriarchy find it difficult to sustain the naturalness of the dichotomy between "masculinity" and "femininity" and the propriety (positive value) of a certain mode of feminine behavior. These times of patriarchal discomfort and confusion are especially useful to explore. That exploration is likely to bear the most fruit if one conducts it with an explicit feminist curiosity, because a feminist curiosity will keep one alert to how even confused ideas about masculinity and femininity can determine who has power and who is marginalized.

Patriarchal confusion often occurs during wartime or when a government is most eager to prepare for war. At first glance, this may seem unlikely. After all, it is during wartime that the masculinity of the protector is most entrenched in its privilege, while the dependent femininity of the grateful protected is most celebrated. But let's look again. And listen. Researchers who have been digging into the complex realities of the American Civil War, World War II, the Vietnam War, and the recent wars in Africa and the Middle East are showing us that policymakers who believe in the naturalness and rightness of a patriarchal social order nonetheless will violate conventional tenets of masculine and feminine difference so that they can use women in new, "nontraditional" ways for the sake of bolstering their war-waging efforts.

Sometimes, in the name of national security preparedness, they may begin violating their own patriarchal rules even before the guns have started firing. But their seeming confusion reaches its most intense level in the later stages of a war, when officials begin to run out of the manpower they most trust—when there are no longer enough young men, especially from those racial and ethnic groups the elites consider "loyal." We saw this happen in apartheid South Africa in the 1980s and in the United States and the Soviet Union during the later years of World War II. At this juncture even die-hard patriarchal officials may become interested in stretching their own and the public's conventional ideas about what "feminine" women can—and should—do. Maybe, on second thought, they can serve as nurses in hospitals near the battle front; maybe they can drive trucks; maybe they can shove artillery shells into large artillery pieces after all, so long as they leave the aiming of the weapons to men. Some semblance of patriarchal war waging is preserved under these dire conditions by policymakers making sure it is only male soldiers who aim the artillery. When policymakers reach this point in their parsing of gender norms, they appear rather desperate.

It is not that these wartime patriarchal officials have shed their patriarchal beliefs and values. Instead, feminist historians have revealed, these officials convince themselves that they can violate their own (and most civilians') gender rules just for the war years and then, in peace time, reestablish the alleged "natural order." In practice, this turns out to be politically risky because it can produce confusion.

As intriguing as it is to explore this militarized patriarchal confusion, some feminist investigators have been wary of devoting intellectual energy to the study of women who become soldiers. These investigators worry that simply by taking seriously the condition of women in the military and such women's experiences and ideas, they unintentionally might help legitimize both the military as a public institution and soldiering as an occupation. The worries of these feminists are rooted in a smart, if pessimistic, analysis that recognizes how seductive militarization can be. It is true that a researcher or journalist (feminist or nonfeminist) can start out neutrally studying a military and can then gradually—unconsciously—start absorbing not only the discourse but the deeper assumptions of that military and of its civilian strategists (Cohn 1987).

However, the militarization of a researcher (or journalist) is not inevitable. To do feminist research of any patriarchal institution and of women living their lives inside that patriarchal institution (e.g., women in corporations, women in legislatures, women in civil service, women in law firms) one does need to acknowledge the risks and thus to cultivate a heightened consciousness of how one's own compassion and imagination, one's own sense of the "good story," one's own sense of "seriousness" each can become militarized in the process of investigating women inside militaries. The telltale sign that one's investigation of women inside militaries is becoming militarized may be that one stops thinking about militarism. One begins to be interested solely in equality and inequality. However, the risks and the effort it takes to avoid those risks are worth taking, for we will never fully understand patriarchy's adaptive qualities and its limits if we avoid studying those women who are trying to pursue their own goals inside such patriarchal institutions.

Now we can return to policymakers' efforts to recruit women into the military *without* losing the support of those members of the public who hold rather restricted notions of proper femininity or proper masculinity and *without* endangering the military's reputation as the place where men can prove their masculinity. One of the well-worn solutions has been to recruit women into the military but to channel them into what the military categorizes as "noncombat" duties such as serving in the medical corps or in the typing pool—or today, serving in the military police, the military guard units, or the military intelligence units. This strategy, which was meant to preserve combat positions for men, placed many U.S. military women on duty in the Abu Ghraib and Guantánamo prisons. This gender-based assignment strategy, officials explain, "frees up men" to do the "real" soldiering. It also preserves the presumably "manly" military occupations for men.

The importance of this gendered assignment strategy means that one should always keep a sharp eye on any military's changing definitions of combat. For instance, even within NATO, whose leaders put so much emphasis on the standardization of weaponry and doctrine, there have been definitional differences in what constitutes a "combat" job and thus where women can or cannot serve alongside men. Moreover, some NATO members have gone further: since the late 1980s, some have eliminated the male-only combat rule altogether. The Dutch led the way, followed closely by the Norwegians and the Canadians.

The Americans and British have been among the most reluctant to give up the male-only combat rule. Thus, it is they who have continued to invest the most political energy in defining and redefining exactly what constitutes "combat." In the 1980s, for instance, the U.S. Army broadened the definition of "combat" to include even the jobs done by electricians and carpenters because, allegedly, carpenters and electricians sometimes were called upon to perform their work near the line of fire. This meant that women soldiers could be excluded from jobs as electricians and carpenters in the name of protecting them from the dangers of combat. One of the facts that made the male-only combat rule seem irrational was that all thirteen of the U.S. military women who were killed in the Gulf War of 1990–1991 were women in what were bureaucratically then defined as "noncombat" positions (Enloe 1993, 2000). During the next decade, under pressure from the Women's Caucus in Congress—and facing the need to have more flexibility in assignments—the army narrowed its definition of "combat."

In most of today's modernized militaries, it is the submarine corps, armored divisions, fighter plane squadrons, paratroops, irregular elite forces such as the U.S. Army's Special Forces, and infantry regiments that remain the inner sanctums of masculinity. Perhaps not surprisingly, these are also the groups within most militaries that are the principal recruiting grounds for future generals and admirals. This is how patriarchy operates in an era of women's rights and globalized modernization.

Under pressure from citizens, many governments have ended male conscription. These are the governments that have been the most determined to enlist more women as volunteers without sacrificing their military's useful masculinized culture. These governments' military strategists have become especially interested in recruiting those young women with high school or even college educations because modern militaries rely on higher literacy and mathematical skills, and in many countries today a higher proportion of young women than young men are completing high school and college. On the other hand, officials don't want women's presence in their military to dilute what they see to be the essence of the institution: its deep affiliation with manliness. So, at the same time as they recruit women to acquire their needed skills, these officials worry that if the military's core masculinized culture is significantly diluted, two dire things will happen. First, a weakened masculinized esprit de corps will produce a military that is a less effective instrument of coercive force. Second, if the popular image of soldiering loses its masculine aura, a lot of young men (potential enlistees) will decide to walk right past the recruiter's office: "Who wants to join an organization that's gone the way of bank telling?" It is with these two patriarchal anxieties (about military effectiveness and about male psychology) in their minds that most military planners and their civilian colleagues go about trying to craft their strategies for recruiting and deploying women to compensate for the men they have lost with the end of male conscription. It has turned out to be a "patriarchal challenge." The resulting practices, not surprisingly, have been confusing, contradictory, and often harmful to the women recruits.

The Women's Research and Education Institute (WREI) and the Miles Foundation are U.S.-based women's advocacy organizations dedicated to reducing sexism inside the U.S. military. Their researchers investigate the results of the U.S. Defense Department's patriarchal confusion. For example, women lawyers at the Miles Foundation revealed that there have been scores of rapes and attempted rapes inside today's American military—sexual assaults by American military men on American military women. The lawyer for one woman soldier refusing to return to duty in Iraq because of repeated sexual harassment she had endured there by her male superiors concluded: "Sexual harassment and sexual assault is an epidemic in the army" (Goldenberg 2006).

Just as noteworthy, most of those charges of assaults seemed to have been cavalierly dismissed or intentionally covered up by senior military officers. After receiving little response from the Pentagon, the Miles Foundation lawyers and the military women (and their parents) they are advising turned to members of Congress. Some of the Republican and Democratic leaders of the Senate Armed Services

Committee, even those Senators often very friendly to the Pentagon, found the evidence of these covered-up assaults disturbing enough that they called special Senate hearings in July 2006 (Miles Foundation; Hillman 2005).

Based in Washington, the WREI has a small but politically savvy team committed to uncovering and making Congress aware of the continued existence of barriers that hinder the careers of American women soldiers: exclusion from combat jobs, sexual harassment, antilesbian "witch hunts," discrimination in promotion evaluations, and neglect of the health and employment needs of the growing number of women veterans. Every two years, the WREI holds a large conference. Since 2000, they have chosen to hold the conference at the new Women's Memorial, a national memorial honoring the contributions that women in the military have made to American society. The WREI invites uniformed active-duty women officers, women veterans, independent civilian scholars, members of congressional staffs, and policymakers. They invite women doing research on women in other countries' militaries—especially researchers from Canada, Britain, and Australia—so that the U.S. experience can be viewed from a global perspective. In recent years, the WREI has also invited women from U.S. and European police and fire departments to speak at the conference, enabling participants to see if there are any commonalities across the various branches of traditionally masculinized uniformed service. For two full days, this diverse gathering explores the everyday practices of sexism—how they are sustained, rationalized, and effectively challenged (Manning 2005).

Neither the women advocates in the Miles Foundation nor those working in the WREI speak openly about "patriarchy." They are intent on persuading members of Congress, Pentagon officials, and the American media to take seriously their findings and their resultant policy recommendations. To achieve this goal, they try to craft a language that will be "heard" by both Republicans and Democrats, by both liberals and conservatives in these overwhelmingly nonfeminist institutions.

The WREI and Miles Foundation researchers and advocates also do not talk about "militarism" or "militarization." Instead, and again in pursuit of influence inside these largely male-dominated institutions, they present their findings and recommendations in the language of classic American "fairness" and "equal opportunity." Yet the findings of both the WREI's and the Miles Foundation's researchers can expose the confusion experienced by patriarchal militarizers.

Nowadays commanders, with civilian policymakers' approval, may assign women to military jobs that many men continue to deem "masculine." This can produce resentment among some men forced to work alongside women in what they consider a male-only preserve. The resentment deepens when those same superiors do not communicate their own genuine commitment to antisexist policies. This combination of ordinary male soldiers' resentment and their superiors' neglect, in turn, can spark sexual harassment, sexualized intimidation, and supervisory inattention by men against those women daring to enter their masculinized sanctum. Civilian women in many countries have experienced similar expressions of hostility in masculinized workplaces: stockbrokerages, legislatures, construction sites, law firms, airlines, sports organizations, newsrooms, and assembly lines (Murphy 2005).

A recent study by the British Ministry of Defence revealed that one in four (25 percent of) British women in the military reported having to deal with offensive male behavior. One in seven had had a "particularly upsetting" experience with their male colleagues, ranging from sexually explicit comments to sexual assault. Half of the women respondents (over 4,000 military women) thought that the British forces had a "sexual harassment problem." In focus groups, most British male soldiers said there was "no problem" (Maley 2006).

In one case that came to the British courts, Corporal Leah Mates, a thirty-year-old soldier with extensive professional military experience, reported being subjected to repeated sexual bullying. When her supervisors treated her reports of the behavior dismissively, Corporal Mates testified, "I now began to understand that the Army is a male preserve, and a woman who tries to establish herself does so at the peril of her health and happiness" (Maley 2006).

Military policymakers have become more reliant on women recruits, yet still seek to reassure the public (and male soldiers) that men in the military will not surrender their "masculinity" when serving with women and that even women who join the military will stay "feminine." Such an insistent reassurance might imply to some listeners that one can masculinize or *de*masculinize any activity. Yes, a soldier in khaki sitting in an office at a typewriter pecking out the commander's memos might have been secure in his masculinity back in the 1940s, but in the early 2000s that is a military job that should be done by a khaki-clad woman. The implication: the differences between women and men are not so intrinsically natural after all. Instead, the differences between what men do and what women do are largely the product of human imagination and decision making. At this point, the patriarchal alarm bells might begin to ring.

> *Dear Worried Patriarchal Public,*
>
> *We are bringing women into this military institution, where you and we know they do not naturally belong, for the sake of national security. National security must take priority over our beliefs about what is natural and what is proper. But don't worry. We know this is a temporary aberration. We, like you, know this is not natural; it is not what we are all fighting for. So we guarantee you that we will rely on this aberration for only a brief time, until we win this war. Then, dear public, having won the war, we will return women to their domestic spheres where they really belong and so the military back to its natural masculinized order and thus the whole social order back to normal. Trust us.*

This is an imagined letter to confused citizens from military planners struggling to cope with personnel shortages. The patriarchal message is that once the war is over, once the threat to national security has been defeated, then the natural and proper gendered social order will be reassuringly restored. This implicit message—sent out in various forms by governments as diverse as the Soviet government, the American government, and the South African government—makes the *post*war years a time to watch carefully. For the reassuring implication is that in the postwar era, women will return—or be returned—to their natural and proper feminine places and roles. In Algeria, Guatemala, Vietnam, El Salvador, Eritrea, and dozens of other countries, these patterns have indeed been repeated: once the imminent threat to national security has receded, women's public space shrinks. Most obvious is the demobilization of women from the ranks of the military. But this demobilization often goes hand in hand with the remasculinization of other spheres of public life such as political parties, factory work, and farm management (Turner 1998; Krosch 2005).

Therefore, it necessary for us as investigators to turn our feminist curiosity to the weeks, months, and even years immediately following the formal end of any foreign or civil war. Those will be the times when—blatantly or subtly—policymakers (and their allies in the media, academia, and business) will try to take steps to terminate the wartime "aberration" and return the military (and thus society) to patriarchal "normality."

That is, to make sense of the gendered dynamics of homegrown and globalized militarization, the postwar years are as interesting to investigate as the war years.

It is when a woman soldier is killed or severely maimed in a combat zone—even if her own job is not strictly speaking a "combat" job—that the norms of patriarchal femininity seem to be most in jeopardy and thus a government's balancing act particularly difficult to sustain.

Look, for instance, at how stories of American women soldiers who have had their legs or arms amputated are told—in the media, on political platforms, in informal conversations. By April 2006, four and a half years into its war in Afghanistan and three years into its war in Iraq, the U.S. government had deployed 99,467 active-duty women soldiers and 37,925 women reservists and National Guard personnel to the two countries (St. George 2006). These women accounted for approximately 12 percent of the total American military forces deployed in Afghanistan and Iraq. Among the 16,600 U.S. soldiers suffering wounds, there were by then 356 wounded women soldiers (St. George 2006). Because of the prevalence of devastating roadside bombs, many of the wounded lost limbs. In a major report on women military amputees, the *Washington Post* portrayed these women as strong, determined, and still in favor of their government's wars. Staff Sergeant Juanita Wilson, who lost her left hand, is an African American mother and wife. Now fitted with an artificial hand, she appears in her army fatigues, describing her plans to stay in the military. Dawn Halfaker, a young white woman, had risen to the rank of captain in the army. She had her right arm amputated up to her shoulder. A woman who sees herself as an athlete, she is portrayed as still jogging and doing yoga, though she worries now about "navigating" dating (St. George 2006). Tammy Duckworth, another army officer, had both her legs amputated. She ran for Congress as a Democrat in Illinois in 2006. She had won the primary but lost the November election. Whereas stories of American male soldiers had been full of descriptions of struggles with depression and unsuccessful surgeries, these women amputees were portrayed as getting on with their lives. This unusual article, which included color photos of the women running with high-tech prostheses, sent two possible implicit messages to its readers: first, don't feel sorry for these women; second, don't shy away from sending women soldiers into combat.

British and Canadian military planners, too, might have breathed a collective sigh of relief when they heard the public reaction in their countries to the deaths of two women soldiers in Iraq and Afghanistan during what their governments also were calling the "global war on terror."

The first was Captain Nichola Goddard, a Canadian woman soldier deployed to southern Afghanistan. She was killed, along with several of her male colleagues, when their armored vehicle was ambushed by Taliban forces who, four years after the U.S.-led military invasion of Afghanistan, were showing signs of resurgence. Nichola Goddard became the first Canadian woman soldier to die in combat since World War II (Krauss 2006).

The other woman soldier to be killed was Flight Lieutenant Sarah-Jayne Mulvihill. While over a hundred British male soldiers had already died in Iraq by May 2006, Sarah-Jayne Mulvihill became the first British woman soldier to be killed in Iraq. No British woman soldier had been killed in action since 1984, when another British woman soldier was killed in the violence in Northern Ireland. Flight Lieutenant Mulvihill was killed in southern Iraq, along with several of her male colleagues, when their helicopter was shot down by insurgents near Basra (Norton-Taylor and Alubedy 2006).

Scores of Afghan and Iraqi women have died in the wars being waged in their countries. However, since no local or occupation authority has tried to keep count of those deaths (estimates of Iraqi civilians killed between 2003 and mid-2006 ranged from 60,000 to 100,000), their numbers are left vague and their names are rarely recorded or made the topics of international news coverage. In both Canada and Britain, the death of each woman soldier was personalized and treated as a major news story.

In Britain, the death of Flight Lieutenant Mulvihill did not mobilize a movement to withdraw women soldiers from combat zones. But it did generate some British media discussion of women's proper roles and the gendered character of fighting wars. Britain has not been one of the pioneers in opening up formerly masculinized military positions for women. Officials of the British government, for example, were slower than their Canadian counterparts and those of several European countries in eliminating the "male-only" combat restriction. It took lawsuits to compel British officials to give British women soldiers proper maternity benefits. And the British Ministry of Defence ended its ban on lesbians and gay men serving openly in the military only when forced to do so in the late 1990s by the European Court of Human Rights.

Nonetheless, the British media's attention to Sarah-Jayne Mulvihill's death in Iraq did escalate the already considerable public criticism of the government's foreign policy. Led by Prime Minister Tony Blair, the British government had chosen to be the foremost political and military international ally of the American government in its invasion and subsequent occupation of Iraq. The first year of the British military's occupation of the largely Shiite region in the south around the city of Basra appeared to go smoothly, with relatively few outbreaks of overt and organized violence. Then in the spring of 2006, that seeming calm disintegrated. British soldiers came under growing pressure from insurgents, and the number of dead British soldiers multiplied. News of the death of a British woman soldier thus appeared to underscore for many British voters this deterioration of the situation in Iraq and its political implications (Lawson 2006).

In Canada, the first woman killed in combat in more than a generation also did not seem to prompt any calls for a reversal of Canada's policy of recruiting substantial numbers of women or deploying them to the front lines of war zones. While by 2005 the British forces had become 8 percent female, the percentage of women in the Canadian forces was almost double that of Britain's, reaching 15 percent. The Canadian forces, compelled to comply with the country's Charter of Rights (adopted in the 1980s), was one of the first countries to eliminate the formal ban on women serving in combat positions and the prohibition on lesbians and gay men serving in the military. Yet the death of Captain Nichola Goddard did send out political ripples. Her death seemed to open up more opportunities for those Canadians skeptical of the government's Afghan policy to voice their concerns. They pressed for more parliamentary debate over Prime Minister Stephen Harper's decision to deploy 2,300 Canadian troops to southern Afghanistan to support the American military's combat operations. In the minds of many Canadians, this policy contradicted a three-decades-old Canadian consensus: Canada's global military role would be one of peacekeeping, not war waging, and therefore Canadian troops would serve overseas only under the multilateral aegis of the United Nations. There was even a monument in the capital, Ottawa, celebrating Canadian soldiers as peacekeepers. No such monument exists in either Britain or the United States. Yet in their 2006 mission to southern Afghanistan, Canadian troops were to be serving as combat soldiers. Neither Captain Goddard nor her Canadian male comrades were wearing the telltale UN peacekeeper's blue helmet. Some Canadians were alarmed: was Canada becoming complicit in globalizing militarization? (Krauss 2006)

WIELDING MASCULINITY INSIDE ABU GHRAIB AND GUANTÁNAMO: THE GLOBALIZED DYNAMICS

In June 2006, two years after the Abu Ghraib scandal broke and set off worldwide consternation, a short article appeared in the *New York Times* reporting that an American army dog handler had been found guilty by a military court-martial. He had been charged with having used his dog to intimidate Iraqi male prisoners being held by the U.S. military at Abu Ghraib (Associated Press 2006). Sergeant Santos A. Cardona was the eleventh American soldier serving in Iraq's infamous Abu Ghraib, a U.S. military jail and interrogation center, to have been convicted of violations of the U.S. military code of conduct. His defense lawyers had argued, unsuccessfully, that Sergeant Cardona was doing only what he had been trained to do and what his military superiors had commanded him to do.

Three of the eleven American soldiers convicted of committing abuses at Abu Ghraib were women, eight were men. All eleven soldiers who were court-martialed and convicted were enlisted personnel or noncommissioned officers. None were higher-ranking officers. None were Washington-based civilian policymakers (Hillman 2005).

The only senior officer to receive an official reprimand and demotion was a woman, General Janis Karpinski. She was the army reserve officer then in charge of the U.S. occupation authority's cobbled-together military prison system in Iraq. Her own telling of the Abu Ghraib story is full of descriptions of wartime unpreparedness, lack of senior command support, autonomous actions by military and CIA interrogators, and routine behaviors in what has become the military's institutional culture of sexism (Karpinski 2005).

On the same June day in 2006 that the *New York Times* reported Sergeant Cardona's conviction, the paper's editors included two other reports that one could read as possibly connected to the short article about Abu Ghraib. First, there was another brief report of the last of the U.S. Army's trials concerning abuses at a U.S. detention center at the Bagram military base in Afghanistan. The last soldier to be prosecuted for abuse and the deaths of prisoners held at Bagram was Private First Class Damien M. Corsetti. He was one of more than a dozen U.S. soldiers—all men—charged with abusing and causing the deaths of Afghan prisoners at Bagram. The military jury acquitted Private Corsetti (Golden 2006).

The Geneva Conventions are international agreements negotiated by governments in the mid-twentieth century. The agreements are not designed so much to reverse militarization as they are intended to globalize the ethics that should guide governments' war-waging behavior. War waging can continue but should be conducted according to these agreed-upon rules. The U.S. government is a signatory to the Geneva Conventions. Prescriptions for the treatment of prisoners captured in wartime is one of the major elements of the Geneva Conventions. That is, a soldier may be in the enemy's forces, but he or she is still a human being and, as a human being, deserves to be treated humanely.

Avoiding these internationally agreed upon requirements to treat prisoners of war humanely was a strategy adopted by U.S. government officials in the name of

- "urgency," coupled with
- "national security," in order to wage
- "the global war on terror."

Those who devised the political rationales, legal interpretations, and bureaucratic strategies for this avoidance were overwhelmingly civilians. They were civilians posted inside the Defense Department, the Justice Department, the White House legal counsel's office, and the office of the vice president (Danner 2004; Mayer 2005a; Mayer 2005b; Mayer 2005c; Mayer 2006).

Witnesses for both the defense and the prosecution at the June 2006 Corsetti court-martial described how the pressures imposed on guards and interrogators at Bagram to get more information from their prisoners increased in late 2002. It was then two months into the U.S.-led military invasion of Afghanistan. President Bush had declared that prisoners captured in Afghanistan were not to be deemed eligible for the international protections guaranteed to enemy combatants under the Geneva Conventions. Many of those male prisoners first detained and questioned at Bagram would soon be flown in large cargo planes—after they had been dressed in orange jump suits, shackled, and had burlap bags placed over their heads—to the detention center the U.S. had recently constructed at its naval base in Guantánamo, Cuba (Lipman forthcoming). The links between Bagram and Guantánamo were being forged.

A year later, those forged links would be extended to Abu Ghraib. Trying to make sense of what happened inside Abu Ghraib in the fall and winter of 2003 turns out to be nearly impossible if one treats Abu Ghraib as an island. It was not an island. It was a link in a globalized chain (Greenberg and Dratel 2005). Among the materials used to weld those chain links—Bagram to Guantánamo, Guantánamo to Abu Ghraib—were American ideas about *feminization.*

Feminization is a process of imposing allegedly feminine characteristics on a person—man or woman—or a group or a kind of activity. Often the goal of feminizing someone (or something) is to lower his (or its) status. Feminization provokes anxiety when particular forms of masculinity are culturally, academically, politically, or economically privileged (Carver 2003; Elias forthcoming). Stitching sneakers for the global market has been feminized in the corporate hope of lowering labor costs. Military nursing has become feminized in an effort to use women in the military without diluting the military's prized image as a masculinized institution. A male candidate running for election against another male candidate may try to gain an advantage with voters by feminizing his opponent—for instance, by portraying his rival as "weak on national security." A male prisoner is feminized when his captors force him to look or act in ways those captors think will make him feel feminine. The presumption motivating his taunters is that a man who is being feminized will become more cooperative out of his sense of shame and helplessness.

In a patriarchal culture—in rich countries and poor countries, in countries with diverse cultural traditions—any person, group, or activity that can be feminized risks losing his or her (or its) influence, authority, and even self-respect. So long as any culture remains patriarchal, then, feminization can be wielded as an instrument of intimidation.

Using a feminist curiosity to make sense of what happened in Abu Ghraib means both investigating any efforts to wield feminization in imprisonment and interrogation and looking for the women in all their various roles. Those roles can be both obvious and obscure. Ann Wright served as an army officer for twenty-nine years and then as a U.S. diplomat before resigning in opposition to the administration's preemptive war. After resigning, Ann Wright decided to use her new independence to find out where all the women were on the broad canvas that became "Abu Ghraib." She found Major General Barbara Fast, chief of military intelligence, serving in the U.S. military command's headquarters in Baghdad. She found Captain Carolyn Wood, a military intelligence officer who had been the leader of the interrogation team in Bagram and then, with her unit, transferred to Abu Ghraib. Wright found two lower-ranking women interrogators deployed to Abu Ghraib, as well as two women employed as interpreters by a civilian contractor, the Titan Company, working with a military intelligence unit inside the prison. Ann Wright also found three Army linguists working in interrogation teams at Guantánamo during 2003 and 2004. She discovered that during these same crucial months at least three other Army women were conducting interrogations at Guantánamo. An unknown number of additional women were serving at Guantánamo at the same time as private contract interrogators. None of these women came forward to stop the abuses they witnessed. Several of them, according to firsthand accounts, helped devise some of the practices meant to humiliate the male prisoners (Wright 2006; Saar 2005).

Is it surprising that there were so many American women inside Bagram, Guantánamo, and Abu Ghraib who, in 2003 and 2004, were playing roles up and down the chain of command as guards, interpreters, and interrogators? Probably not. After all, over the past two decades, in devising gender strategies for recruiting women while still maintaining the military's masculinized core—combat—officials of the U.S. Defense Department had channeled women soldiers into not just nursing and administration but such seemingly noncontroversial jobs as military police, military interpreters, and intelligence. By 2004, women, who made up only 15 percent of total U.S. Army personnel, represented 22 percent of military police and 25 percent of military interrogators (Wright 2006).

Still, using a feminist curiosity to make sense of Abu Ghraib, Bagram, and Guantánamo allows one to do more than look for where the women are—as revealing as that exploration is. Using a feminist curiosity prompts one to also pursue the answer to a question that most commentators fail to ask: what are the causes and consequences of wielding ideas about masculinity and femininity?

Feminization has been used during the Afghanistan and Iraq wars mainly by American militarized men (civilian and military), but with the complicity and sometimes the direct involvement of a handful of American militarized women. Evidence gathered thus far suggests that feminization was intended by its wartime wielders to humiliate and thereby gain information from foreign men, mostly men identified by their American captors as "Muslim," " dangerous," and "the enemy." As they were transported by U.S. officials from Washington to Bagram to Guantánamo to Abu Ghraib, these practices of coercive feminization might be thought of as being *globally militarized.*

Back at Private Corsetti's June 2006 barely reported court-martial, defense witnesses sought to undercut the prosecution's case against Corsetti by noting that there were almost-daily phone calls to interrogators at Bagram from their civilian Defense Department superiors in Washington. Their superiors were infused with a sense of urgency. They demanded quick results from the interrogations being conducted at the Bagram base. The witnesses recalled how this pressure from Washington officials served to increase the aggressiveness of the physical tactics that Bagram soldiers and interrogators used on prisoners deemed uncooperative (Golden 2006). The jury seemed convinced.

American military interrogators' and guards' adoption of both painful "stress positions" and feminization to intimidate captive men can be traded globally, just as rifles can be traded globally, just as ideas about national security and creating "cheap labor" can be traded globally.

American male and female soldiers serving during late 2003 and early 2004 as prison guards in Abu Ghraib became the best known actors in this fast-globalizing drama. As individuals, they seemed far from being global players. They appeared quite parochial and isolated. The photographs that showed them deliberately humiliating and torturing scores of Iraqi men held in detention and under interrogation were taken apparently for their own private amusement, not for prime-time television or headline stories. But their audience expanded beyond their wildest dreams—or nightmares. Between April and June 2004, millions of viewers were looking at these private photos: American soldiers smiling broadly as they appeared to be taking enormous pleasure in frightening and humiliating their wartime Iraqi charges.

Most people who saw these photographs can still describe the scenes. An American male soldier standing in a self-satisfied pose, facing his army colleague holding the camera with his arms crossed and wearing surgical blue rubber gloves, a sign that this abuse was occurring in the age of AIDS. In front of him, we, the globalized viewers of these photographs, could see an American woman soldier smiling at the camera as she leaned on top of a pile of naked Iraqi men who were being forced to contort themselves into a human pyramid.

Other pictures whizzed around the planet. An American woman soldier, again smiling, holding an Iraqi male prisoner on a leash. An American woman soldier pointing to a naked Iraqi man's genitals, apparently treating them as a joke. American male soldiers intimidating naked Iraqi male prisoners with snarling guard dogs. An Iraqi male prisoner standing alone on a box, his head covered with a hood and electrical wires attached to different parts of his body. An Iraqi male prisoner forced to wear women's underwear. Not pictured, but substantiated, were Iraqi men forced to masturbate and to simulate oral sex with each other, as well as an Iraqi woman prisoner coerced by several American male soldiers into kissing them (Hersh 2004).

Few of the U.S. government's official investigators or the mainstream news commentators used feminist insights to make sense of what went on in the prison (Strasser 2004; Danner 2004). The result, I think, is that we have not really gotten to the bottom of the Abu Ghraib story. This, in turn, could undercut our attempts to understand how militarization can lead to torture.

This omission of a feminist analysis in investigations of Abu Ghraib—and of abusive actions inside Bagram and Guantánamo, *as well as* the connections forged between these places—could also limit our attempts to implement those changes that can enforce globalized treaties and conventions intended to either roll back militarization or at least reduce its harmful effects.

One place to start employing a feminist set of tools is to explain why one American woman soldier in particular—not even a guard, just a low-ranking clerk visiting the cell block the night the photos were taken—captured the attention of so many media editors and ordinary viewers and readers: the then twenty-one-year-old enlisted army reservist Lynndie England, now a single mother serving a sentence in a military prison.

Why didn't the name of Charles Graner, the apparent cell-block ringleader of the photographed abuses become as well known? More important to ask: why didn't the name of General Geoffrey Miller become globally known? General Geoffrey Miller was the commander of Guantánamo and when he was sent to Iraq, became the carrier of Washington's message from Guantánamo to Abu Ghraib—a message that this was a time demanding a sense of urgency, an urgency that called for more aggressive techniques in interrogations of Iraqi prisoners held in Abu Ghraib (Hersh 2004). The fact that neither Graner's nor, especially, Miller's name did become as familiar reflects the gendering not just of the abuse but also of the political consciousnesses of Americans and news consumers around the world: women in presumably masculinized places, such as a military prison in a war zone, make a better "story."

Several things proved shocking to the millions of viewers of the clandestine prison photos. First, the Abu Ghraib scenes suggested

99

there existed a gaping chasm between, on the one hand, the Bush administration's claim that its military invasion and overthrow of the brutal Saddam Hussein regime would bring a civilizing sort of "freedom" to the Iraqi people and, on the other hand, the seemingly barbaric treatment that American soldiers were willfully meting out to Iraqis held in captivity without trial. Second, it was shocking to witness such blatant abuse of imprisoned detainees by soldiers representing a government that had passed its own antitorture laws and had signed both the international Geneva Conventions against mistreatment of wartime combatants and the UN Convention against Torture and Other Cruel, Inhuman or Degrading Treatment or Punishment (sometimes referred to simply as the "Convention Against Torture").

Yet there was a third source of shock that prompted scores of early media commentaries and intense conversations among ordinary viewers: seeing women engage in torture. Of the seven American soldiers initially court-martialed (and eleven soldiers eventually court-martialed), all low-ranking army reserve military police guards, three were women. Somehow, the American male soldier in the blue surgical gloves (Charles Graner) was not shocking to most viewers and so did not inspire much private consternation or a stream of op-ed columns. Women, by contrast, were conventionally expected by most editors and news watchers to appear in wartime as mothers and wives of soldiers, occasionally as military nurses and truck mechanics, and most often as victims of wartime violence. Women were not—according to the conventional presumption— supposed to be the wielders of violence and certainly not the perpetrators of torture. When those deeply gendered presumptions were turned upside down, many people felt a sense of shock. "This is awful; how could this have happened?"

Private First Class Lynndie England, the young female military clerk (not a guard) photographed holding the man on a leash, thus became the source of intense public curiosity. The news photographers could not restrain themselves two months later, in early August 2004, from showing England in her camouflaged army maternity uniform when she appeared at Fort Bragg for her pretrial hearing. She had become pregnant as a result of her sexual liaison with another enlisted reservist while on duty in Abu Ghraib. Her sexual partner was Charles Graner. Yet Charles Graner's name was scarcely mentioned. He apparently was doing what men are expected to do in wartime: have sex and wield violence. The public's curiosity and its lack of curiosity thus matched its pattern of shock. All three—curiosity, lack of curiosity, and shock—were conventionally gendered. Using a feminist investigatory approach, one should find this lack of public and media curiosity about Charles Graner just as revealing as the public's and media's fascination with Lynndie England.

Yet more than Charles Graner was pushed aside. The government policymaking that implicitly approved the use of torture was never put on trial. In fact, one reporter who, with a handful of her colleagues followed the Abu Ghraib trials for months, all the way through to the trial of Lynndie England (the last of the low-ranking Abu Ghraib soldiers to be tried) and heard Lynndie England's sentence pronounced in the court room at Fort Hood, Texas, in September 2005, noted how narrow the focus remained throughout all the trials. Bigger issues were deemed irrelevant (Wypijewski 2006). In fact, it was considered quite exceptional when General Geoffrey Miller, the Guantánamo commander who had brought the message to Iraq in the fall of 2003 that pressure on captured suspected insurgents needed to be increased, appeared briefly at just one of the many court sessions. No senior civilian officials from the Defense or Justice Department made any appearances. This legalistic narrowing of the focus served to normalize in the minds of many ordinary people those government interrogation policies and the resultant practice of inflicting physical pain and feminized humiliation that flowed from them.

Responding to the torrent of Abu Ghraib stories coming out of Iraq during the spring and summer of 2004, President George W. Bush and Secretary of Defense Donald Rumsfeld, the president's appointee, tried to reassure the public that the abusive behavior inside the prison was not representative of America, nor did it reflect the Bush administration's own foreign policies. Rather, the Abu Ghraib abuses were the work of "rogue" soldiers, a "few bad apples."

The "bad apple" explanation always goes like this: the institution is working fine, its values are appropriate, its internal dynamics are of a sort that sustain positive values, along with respectful, produc-

tive behavior. Thus, according to the "bad apple" explanation, nothing needs to be reassessed or reformed in the way the organization
works; all that needs to happen to stop the abuse is to prosecute and
remove those few individuals who refused to play by the established
rules. Sometimes this may be true. Some listeners to the administration's "bad apple" explanation, however, weren't reassured. They
wondered if the Abu Ghraib abuses were not produced by just a few
bad apples found in a solid, reliable barrel but instead were produced by an essentially "bad barrel." They also wondered whether
this "barrel" embraced not only the Abu Ghraib prison, but the
larger U.S. military, intelligence, and civilian command structures
(Hersh 2004; Human Rights Watch 2004).

What makes a "barrel" go bad? That is, what turns an organization, an institution, or a whole system into one that ignores, perhaps
even fosters, abusive behavior by the individuals operating inside it?
This question is relevant for every workplace, every political system,
every international alliance. Here, too, feminists have been working
hard over the past three decades to develop a curiosity and a set of
analytical tools with which we can all answer this important question. So many of us today live much of our lives within complex
organizations, large and small—workplaces, local and national governments, health care systems, criminal justice systems, international organizations. Feminist researchers have revealed that
virtually all organizations are gendered; that is, all organizations are
shaped by the ideas about, and daily practices of wielding, norms of
masculinity and femininity (Bunster-Burotto 1985; Ehrenreich
2004; Enloe 2000; Whitworth 2004; Burke 2004). Ignoring the
workings of gender, feminist investigators have found, makes it impossible for us to explain accurately what makes any organization
"tick." That failure makes it impossible for us to hold an organization accountable.

Yet most of the long official reports on the Abu Ghraib abuse
scandal were written by people who ignored these feminist organizational lessons. They acted as if the dynamics of masculinity and
femininity among low-level police and high-level policymakers
made no difference. That assumption is very risky.

A series of U.S. Senate hearings, along with a string of Defense
Department investigations, tried to explain what went wrong in Abu

Ghraib and why. The most authoritative of the Defense Department reports were the "Taguba Report," the "Fay/Jones Report" (both named after generals who headed these investigations), and the "Schlesinger Report" (named after a civilian former secretary of defense who chaired this investigatory team) (Human Rights Watch 2004; Jehl 2004; Lewis and Schmitt 2004; Schmitt 2004; Taguba 2004). In addition, the CIA conducted its own investigation, since its officials were deeply involved in interrogating—and often hiding in secret prisons—captured Afghans and Iraqis. Moreover, there were several human rights groups and journalists that published their own findings in 2004.

Together they offered a host of valuable clues as to why this institutional "barrel" had gone bad. First, investigators discovered that lawyers inside the Defense and Justice departments as well as the White House, acting on instructions from their civilian superiors, produced interpretations of the Geneva Conventions and U.S. law that deliberately shrank the definitions of "torture" down so far that American military and CIA personnel could use techniques that otherwise would have been deemed violations of U.S. and international law.

Second, investigators found that General Geoffrey Miller was sent by Secretary Rumsfeld to Iraq in September 2003, where General Miller recommended that American commanders overseeing military prison operations in Iraq start employing the aggressive interrogation practices that were being used on Afghan and Arab male prisoners at Guantánamo. Somewhat surprisingly, General Miller later was named by the Pentagon to head the Abu Ghraib prison in the wake of the scandal.

Third, investigators discovered that the intense, persistent pressure imposed on military intelligence personnel by the Defense Department to generate information about who was launching insurgent assaults on the U.S. occupying forces encouraged those military intelligence officers in turn to put pressure on the military police guarding prisoners to "soften up" the men in their cell blocks. This undercut the military police's own chain of command. At the top of that command chain was a female army general, Janice Karpinski, who claimed that her authority over her military police personnel had been undermined by intrusive military intelligence

103

officers. This policy change, the U.S. government's own investigators concluded, dangerously blurred the valuable line between military policing and military interrogating. Finally, investigators found that nonmilitary personnel, including CIA operatives and outside contractors hired by the CIA and the Pentagon, were involved in the Abu Ghraib military interrogations in ways that may have fostered a string of reinforcing assumptions that the legal limitations on employing excessive force could be treated cavalierly, seeming to have sent the message: "We're under threat, repelling this threat is urgent, the Geneva Conventions or other legal niceties are slowing down our efforts to act with urgency."

Using our feminist curiosity leads us to ask several questions that the U.S. government's investigators failed to ask:

- Did it matter who the women were inside the prison and up and down the larger American military and intelligence hierarchies—low-level police reservists, a captain in the military intelligence unit, a general advising the chief U.S. commander in Iraq? Investigators apparently didn't ask.
- Did the nature of the daily personal relationships between the military police*men*, including Charles Graner, and their female colleagues—who were a minority at Abu Ghraib—matter? The official investigators didn't seem to think that asking this question would yield any insights.
- Was it significant that so many of the abuses perpetrated on the Iraqi male prisoners were deliberately sexualized, designed to feminize and thus humiliate the prisoners? Was hooding a male prisoner the same (in motivation and in result) as forcing him to simulate oral sex? No one seemed to judge these questions to be pertinent.
- Was it at all relevant that Charles Graner, the oldest and apparently most influential of the low-ranking guards charged, had been accused of physical intimidation by his former wife? No questions asked, no answers forthcoming.
- Was subtle pressure to appear "manly" in a time of war placed on the lawyers in the Defense and Justice departments and in the White House who were ordered to draft guidelines to permit U.S. officials to sidestep the Geneva Conventions outlaw-

ing torture? This question too seems to have been left on the investigative teams' shelves to gather dust.

Since the mid-1970s, feminists have been introducing new questions to pose and crafting skills to explain when and why organizations become arenas for sexist abuse. One of the great contributions of the work done by what is often referred to as the "Second Wave" of the international women's movement (that is, feminist activism of the 1960s to 1990s) has been to shed light on what breeds sex discrimination and sexual harassment inside organizations otherwise as dissimilar as a factory, a stockbrokerage, a legislature, a university, a student movement, and a military (Bowers 2004; Kwon 2000; Ogasawara 1998; Stockford 2004; Whitworth 2004; Murphy 2005). All of the authors of the reports on Abu Ghraib talked about a "climate," an "environment," or a "culture," having been created inside Abu Ghraib that fostered abusive acts. The conditions inside Abu Ghraib were portrayed as having been part of a climate of "confusion," of "chaos." It is important to note that it was feminists who gave us this innovative concept of organizational climate.

When trying to figure out why women employees in some organizations were subjected to sexist jokes, unwanted advances, and retribution for not going along with the jokes or not accepting those advances, feminist lawyers, advocates, and scholars began to look beyond the formal policies and the written rules. They explored something more amorphous but just as potent, and maybe even more so: the set of unofficial presumptions that shapes workplace interactions between men and men and between men and women. They followed the bread crumbs to the casual, informal interactions between people up and down the organization's ladder. They investigated who drinks with whom after work, who sends sexist jokes to whom over office e-mail, who pins up which sorts of pictures of women in their lockers or next to the coffee machine. And they looked into what those people in authority did *not* do. They discovered that *inaction* is a form of action: "turning a blind eye" is itself a form of action. Inaction sends out signals to everyone in the organization about what is condoned. Feminists labeled these webs of presumptions, informal interactions, and deliberate inaction as an organization's "climate." As feminists argued successfully in court, it is not sufficient for a stockbrokerage or a college to include anti-sexual-harassment guidelines in its official handbook; employers have to take explicit steps to create a workplace climate in which women are treated with fairness and respect.

By 2004, this feminist explanatory concept—organizational "climate"—had become so accepted by so many analysts that their debt to feminists had been forgotten. Generals Taguba, Jones, and Fay, as well as former defense secretary Schlesinger, may never have taken a women's studies course, but when they were assigned the job of investigating Abu Ghraib they were drawing on the ideas and investigatory skills crafted for them by feminists.

However, more worrisome than the failure by such investigators to acknowledge their intellectual and political debts was their ignoring the feminist lessons that went hand in hand with the concept of "climate." The first lesson: to make sense of any organization, we always must dig deep into the group's dominant presumptions about femininity and masculinity. The second lesson: we need to take seriously the experiences of women as they try to adapt to, or sometimes resist, those dominant gendered presumptions—not because all women are angels, but because paying close attention to women's ideas and actions will shed light on why men with power act the way they do.

It is not as if the potency of ideas about masculinity and femininity had been totally absent from the U.S. military's thinking. Between 1991 and 2004, there had been a string of military scandals that had compelled even those American senior officials who preferred to look the other way to face sexism straight on. The first stemmed from the September 1991 gathering of American navy pilots at a Hilton hotel in Las Vegas. Male pilots (all officers), fresh from their victory in the first Gulf War, lined a hotel corridor and physically assaulted every woman who stepped off the elevator. They made the "mistake" of assaulting a woman navy helicopter pilot who was serving as an aide to an admiral. Within months, members of Congress and the media were telling the public about "Tailhook"—why it happened and who tried to cover it up (Office of the Inspector General 2003). Close on the heels of the navy's "Tailhook" scandal came the army's Aberdeen training base sexual harassment scandal, followed by other revelations of gay bashing, sexual harassment, and rapes by American male military personnel (Enloe 1993, 2000).

Then in September 1995, the rape of a local school girl by two American male marines and a sailor in Okinawa sparked public demonstrations, the formation of new Okinawan women's advocacy groups, and more congressional investigations in the United States. At the start of the twenty-first century, American media began to notice the patterns of international trafficking in Eastern European and Filipino women around American bases in South Korea, prompting official embarrassment in Washington (embarrassment that had not been demonstrated earlier when American base commanders turned a classic "blind eye" to a prostitution industry organized locally to service those commanders' own male soldiers, because it employed "just" local South Korean women). And in 2003, three new American military sexism scandals caught Washington policymakers' attention: four American male soldiers returning from combat missions in Afghanistan murdered their female partners at Fort Bragg, North Carolina; a pattern of sexual harassment and rape by male cadets of female cadets—and superiors' refusal to treat these acts seriously—was revealed at the U.S. Air Force Academy; and at least sixty American women soldiers returning from tours of duty in Kuwait and Iraq testified that they had been sexually assaulted by their male colleagues there—once again, with senior officers choosing inaction and advising the American women soldiers to "get over it" (Jargon 2003; Lutz and Elliston 2004; Miles Foundation 2004; Moffeit and Herder 2004).

Carol Burke, a professor of folklore, taught at the U.S. Naval Academy at Annapolis. When the evidence of abuses perpetrated in Abu Ghraib started to become news, she immediately drew the parallels between what had gone on inside the prison and what she herself had witnessed routinely among American male cadets at the naval academy: men using feminized rituals of hazing to try to humiliate other male cadets, which simultaneously reinforced the collective contempt with which anything "tainted" with femininity was held. Even the use of women's underwear and the coerced sexual acts were identical (Burke 2004, 2006).

So it should have come as no surprise to senior uniformed and civilian policymakers seeking to make sense of the abuses perpe-

107

trated in Abu Ghraib that a culture of sexism had come to permeate many sectors of U.S. military life. If they had thought about what they had all learned in the last thirteen years—from Tailhook, Aberdeen, Fort Bragg, Okinawa, South Korea, and the U.S. Air Force Academy—they should have put the workings of masculinity and femininity at the top of their investigatory agendas. They should have made feminist curiosity one of their own principal tools. Perhaps Tillie Fowler did suggest to her colleagues that they think about these military scandals when they began to delve into Abu Ghraib. A former Republican congresswoman from Florida, Tillie Fowler had been a principal investigator on the team that looked into the rapes (and their cover-ups) at the U.S. Air Force Academy. Because of her leadership in that role, Fowler was appointed to the commission headed by James Schlesinger investigating Abu Ghraib. Did she raise this comparison between the Air Force Academy case and Abu Ghraib? If she did, did her male colleagues take her suggestion seriously?

Perhaps ultimately the investigators did not make use of the feminist lessons and tools because they imagined that the lessons of Tailhook, Aberdeen, Fort Bragg, Okinawa, South Korea, and the Air Force Academy were relevant only when all the perpetrators of sexual abuse are men and all the victims are women. Perhaps they ignored their knowledge of the sexualized hazing practices common in American military organizations (and in fraternities and sports teams at American colleges) because, after all, those could be dismissed as "boys being boys" and could be imagined as having no serious consequences on either the men being hazed or the women implicitly being denigrated.

The presence of Lynndie England and the other women in Abu Ghraib's military police unit, they might have assumed, made the feminist tools sharpened in those earlier gendered military scandals inappropriate for their current investigation. But the lesson of Tailhook and the other military scandals was *not* that the politics of masculinity and femininity matter only when men are the perpetrators and women are the victims. Instead, the deeper lesson of all those other military scandals is that we must always ask "has this organization (or this system of interlocking organizations) become masculinized in ways that privilege certain forms of masculinity, feminize its opposition, and trivialize most forms of femininity?"

With this core gender question in mind, we might uncover significant dynamics operating in Abu Ghraib and in the American military and civilian organizations that were supposed to be supervising the prison's personnel. American military police and their military and CIA intelligence colleagues might have been guided by their *own* masculinized fears of humiliation when they forced Iraqi men to go naked for days, to wear women's underwear, and to masturbate in front of each other and American women guards. That is, the Americans' belief in an allegedly "exotic," frail Iraqi masculinity, fraught with fears of nakedness and homosexuality, might not have been the chief motivator for the American police and intelligence personnel; it may have been their own homegrown American sense of masculinity's fragility—how easily manliness can be feminized—that prompted them to craft these prison humiliations. Either belief could encourage the guards to wield feminization as a technique of prisoner humiliation. In this distorted masculinized scenario, the presence of women serving as military police might have proved especially useful. Choreographing the women guards' feminized roles so that they could act as ridiculing feminized spectators of male prisoners might have been imagined to intensify the demasculinizing demoralization. As histories of international conflicts in Vietnam, Rwanda, and Western Europe have revealed, dominant men trying to use women in ways that undermine the masculinized self-esteem of rival men is not new.

What about the American women soldiers themselves? In the U.S. military of 2004, women constituted 15 percent of active duty personnel, 17 percent of all reserves and the National Guard, and a surprising 24 percent of the army reserves alone. From the very time these particular young women joined this military police unit, they, like their fellow male recruits, probably sought to fit into the group. If the unit's evolving culture—perhaps fostered by their superiors for the sake of "morale" and "unit cohesion"—was one that privileged a certain form of masculinized humor, racism, and bravado, each woman would have had to decide how to deal with that. At least some of the women reservists might have decided to join in, to play the roles assigned to them in order to gain the hoped-for reward of male acceptance. The fact that the Abu Ghraib prison was grossly understaffed during the fall of 2003 (too few guards for the spiraling numbers of Iraqi detainees), that it was isolated from other military operations, and that its residents endured daily and nightly mortar attacks would only serve to intensify the pressures on each soldier to gain acceptance from those unit members who seemed to represent the group's dominant masculinized culture. And what about the fact that Lynndie England entered into a sexual liaison with Charles Graner? We need to treat this as more than merely a "lack of discipline." Looking back on the masculinized and sexualized climate inside the both internally troubled and externally besieged prison, Janis Karpinski, the army reserve general in charge of the prison, recalled how, over the years of her career, she had seen so many young women soldiers "seek protection" from older, more senior male soldiers, usually with those men more than willing to serve as their female subordinates' "protectors" (Karpinski forthcoming). It would be more useful to ask about the cause and effect dynamics between these soldiers' sexual behaviors and their abuses of Iraqi prisoners (including the staged photographs). Feminists have taught us never to brush off sexual relations as if they have nothing to do with organizational and political practices.

Then there is the masculinization of the military interrogators' organizational culture, the masculinization of the CIA's field operatives, and the ideas about "manliness" shaping the entire U.S. political system. Many men and women—lawyers, generals, cabinet members, elected officials—knew full well that aggressive interrogation techniques violated both the spirit and the language of the Geneva Conventions, the UN Convention against Torture, and U.S. federal law against torture. Yet during the months of waging wars in Afghanistan and Iraq, most of these men and women kept silent. Feminists have taught us always to be curious about silence. Thus, we need to ask: did any of the American men involved in interrogations keep silent because they were afraid of being labeled "soft" or "weak," thereby jeopardizing their status as "manly" men? We need also to discover if any of the women who knew better kept silent because they were afraid that they would be labeled "feminine," thus risking being deemed by their colleagues to be untrustworthy outsiders.

We are not going to get to the bottom of the tortures perpetrated by Americans at Abu Ghraib unless we make use of a feminist curiosity and unless we revisit the feminist lessons derived from the scandals that have been revealed at the Tailhook convention, Fort Bragg, the U.S. Naval Academy, Okinawa, and the Air Force Academy. A feminist curiosity, combined with those lessons, might shed a harsh light on an entire American military institutional culture and maybe even the climate of contemporary American political life. That military culture and that political climate together have profound implications for both Americans and for all those citizens in countries where the U.S. military is being held up as a model to emulate as they modernize their own armed forces. Those citizens being encouraged to adopt the American military's culture and political climate—in Eastern Europe's newest members of NATO, as well as in South Korea, Japan, the Philippines, Afghanistan, and Iraq—might find it valuable to consider these feminist-informed lessons.

Let's return to that June 2006 newspaper. There was a third article in that paper that a reader, sipping a morning cup of coffee in the safety of her or his own kitchen, might have noticed. The *New York Times* editors made this article much more prominent than the others. This article dealt with the rapidly unfolding story of assaults by U.S. male marines in the Iraqi town of Haditha on November 19, 2005.

The alleged assaults took place a year after Abu Ghraib dominated the world's headlines and two years after the infamous photos were taken by gloating American guards. Eight months later investigations into what happened that November in Haditha began to become known to the public. Now, in mid-2006, a story was unfolding that suggested that a group of marines retaliated violently after one of their fellow marines had been killed by a roadside bomb. They allegedly killed perhaps as many as two dozen Iraqi civilians, including an old man in a wheelchair, women inside their own homes, and children as young as four years old. Later, seemingly with the support of some of their superior officers, these marines claimed that the Iraqis had been killed by an insurgent's bomb or in intense combat. Forensic evidence that was later revealed, however, suggested that these twenty-four Iraqi civilians had been shot at close range by the marines (Broder et al. 2006).

Haditha is a town in the sparsely populated Iraqi province of Anbar. Over the past two decades Anbar's local culture had become both more militarized and more masculinized; those two intertwined processes, already underway, seemed to speed up even more following the U.S. invasion in 2003, as the predominantly Sunni population mobilized to fight its own insurgency against the U.S. military occupation. In November 2005, these Iraqi processes met another process of masculinized militarization head on—this process was American. According to some American observers, the U.S. Marines, who had just rotated into Anbar, replacing the previous army troops there, were determined to impose a tougher, more masculinized operational discipline on the rebellious province. The U.S. Marines' culture of masculinity would replace—and presumably be more effective against the insurgents than—the U.S. Army's allegedly weaker culture of masculinity (Burns 2006). A subsequent investigation by a senior army commander found that marine officers, including those not physically on the scene that deadly November day, had laid the cultural groundwork for the massacre: they had created a particular "climate." One Pentagon official explained the cultural message that the marine officers had sent down through the ranks about how American soldiers should view Iraqis in Anbar: "In their eyes, they didn't believe anyone was innocent . . . . Either you were an active participant, or you were complicit" (Cloud 2006).

"Haditha" was becoming shorthand for another stew of gendered globalized militarized dynamics.

Some members of the U.S. Congress compared the November 2005 massacre at Haditha and its apparent cover-up to the U.S. military massacre of civilians over thirty years ago, in 1968, in the Vietnamese village of My Lai. Other American legislators, trying to assess preliminary evidence of the seemingly out-of-control and violent behavior of lower-ranking soldiers and the attempted cover-ups by superiors, drew analogies to a more recent scandal, Abu Ghraib (Oppel 2006).

All of these news stories—some making the front page, others buried by editors on the inside pages—were breaking, furthermore, at the same time as international legal experts were calling on the

U.S. government to close down its military prison and interrogation center in Guantánamo. European legal scholars and investigators had concluded that U.S. military practices at Guantánamo stood in violation of the agreed-upon international norms governing warfare and rules protecting human rights (Sciolino 2006).

Thus, evidence gathered between 2004 and 2006 suggested that the U.S. militarized practices at Guantánamo, at Bagram, and at Abu Ghraib were linked, gendered, and globalized.

In April 2004, a year after the U.S. government had launched its massive military invasion of Iraq, a series of shocking photographs of American soldiers abusing Iraqi prisoners began appearing on television news programs, the front pages of newspapers, and Internet sites around the world. The revelations of Abu Ghraib quickly took on the attributes of a globalized event.

Abu Ghraib was globalized, first, in that it exposed actions by military personnel and their civilian superiors that were in blatant violation of internationally agreed-upon norms of state behavior—norms written into international law and ratified by the U.S. government. Many people around the globe for the first time read paragraphs of the UN Convention against Torture, and Other Cruel, Inhuman or Degrading Treatment or Punishment, even though it had been adopted in 1984 and signed by their governments in their name. While often referred to simply as the "Convention Against Torture," its full title makes clear its far broader prohibition. The U.S. government, on behalf of all U.S. citizens, signed the Convention. The impetus for its creation in the early 1980s was the international revulsion at the news of the use of torture by military regimes in Chile and Argentina—something that was not uncommon in dozens of other countries ruled by authoritarian and militarized governments, which claimed that enemies within and without could be dealt with only by extraordinary and, if necessary, violent state methods. An international consensus rejected this justification. The Convention against Torture was the product of that historic consensus (Sands 2005).

Second, Abu Ghraib became globalized in that it sparked a worldwide discussion—one that is still going on today—about the ethics of waging war, about the definitions of torture, about the accountability of intelligence services, about urgency, about fear. During the spring and summer of 2004, as the evidence of what had occurred in the cell blocks of Abu Ghraib almost a year earlier mounted, ordinary citizens found themselves talking with friends about "sexual humiliation," "sleep deprivation," "stress positions," and "psychological torture." Many listened to, or read for the first time, detailed discussions by legal and political experts about what counts as "torture," whether torture "works," how ordinary individuals could be desensitized (and by whom) to the point that they could become torturers, and how torture undermines democratic cultures and the rule of law. In the age of satellite television and around-the-clock Internet communication, this became a globalized conversation.

Third, what American personnel—military and militarized—had done inside Abu Ghraib was globalized in the sense that people from scores of countries began to see themselves as having a stake in understanding and critiquing the causes and actions that were gradually revealed. Not everyone agreed that such critical national self-reflection was necessary. In fact, there were people who argued that since the September 11, 2001, attacks, preventing terrorism justified all means of capture, detention, and interrogation. The stakes were too high, they contended, to allow the norms of legal conventions and formal treaties to get in the way of effective prevention. On the other side, often in the same country, there were people who felt that the stakes were too high to treat Abu Ghraib as merely a one-country story. They saw the fundamental character of the twenty-first century's international political system as being at stake: would everyone revert to imagining that abusive militarism in one country did not jeopardize the cultures of law and human rights and decency in all others, especially when the government claiming the exception was itself so culturally and militarily influential?

This stream of globalized thinking was especially meaningful in those countries, such as Chile, Argentina, South Africa, Guatemala, Greece, Turkey, and South Korea, where torture committed by militarized regimes was still fresh in the minds of many citizens and where the work to undo the cultural and structural damage inflicted by those authoritarian regimes was still going on even twenty years after the generals had been forced to relinquish their power.

Fourth, in the months and years following the disclosure of the prisoner abuse, the Abu Ghraib scandal became globalized because the very setting in which the abuses occurred was internationalized:

one state, the United States, had preemptively invaded the territory of another state, Iraq, with the officially expressed intent of imposing *international* norms of democratic political and legal behavior on that state. That justification itself militarized every revelation of abusive behavior by any American low- or high-ranking soldier or civilian in the course of waging war in Iraq.

Fifth, and last, the abusive treatment of Iraqi prisoners in Abu Ghraib turned out to be globalized in the sense that American defense and intelligence officials had purposefully transported ideas around the world—ideas about who was not worthy of prisoners' rights, ideas about whose interrogation was "urgent," and ideas about what techniques of interrogation were allowable and "effective."

Thus, Lynndie England was never "the story." She is interesting. She deserves to be fully understood. But so too do Janis Karpinski, Charles Graner's former wife, General Barbara Fast, Captain Carolyn Wood, and the women who served as military and contract interrogators and interpreters in both Guantánamo and Abu Ghraib. Paying attention to diverse militarized women's actions, motivations, assumptions, and immediate as well as distant relationships to male senior commanders and male civilian policymakers can help us see how militarized feminization operates, who wields it, who is complicit in it and why, whom it serves, and what larger cultural goals it promotes.

Furthermore, it is by tracking the gendered assumptions about how to wield feminization to humiliate male prisoners inside Abu Ghraib, *not* in isolation, but with the understanding that those assumptions were linked to the ideas, assumptions, and policies shaping detention and interrogation practices at Bagram and Guantánamo—and the unknown number of secret prisons used by the U.S. government around the world—that we are likely to get a clearer picture of why "Abu Ghraib" happened—and whether it will happen again.

Note

An earlier, quite different, version of this chapter was published as: "Wielding Masculinity Inside Abu Ghraib," *Asian Journal of Women's Studies* 10, no. 3 (September 2004): 235–243.

DEMILITARIZING A SOCIETY IN A GLOBALIZED WORLD; *OR*, DO YOU WEAR "CAMO"?

The Women of Color Resource Center (WCRC) isn't what most experts think of as a site of research on militarization and demilitarization. But that oversight may be due to many militarization experts' narrow views of "expertise." The WCRC is an energetic organization located in downtown Oakland, California, that develops programs for Asian American, African American, Native American, and Latina women in the San Francisco Bay Area. As the director of the WCRC's small antimilitarism project, Christine Ahn wanted to find a topic that would engage these young women in thinking about their own possible complicity in the processes of militarization. In 2004, she began mulling over the meanings of "camo." Camo is the popular nickname for the fashion of turning the military's camouflaged designs into tank tops, shorts, pants, knapsacks, even condoms. Ahn wondered whether the many young people she knew who were buying and wearing this "hip" fashion—her peers—had thought about the implications of their style choices. Christine Ahn went into action. She organized what might have been the first-ever antimilitarism fashion show.

In late May 2005, the WCRC took over the refurbished theater in downtown Oakland. By 8:00 p.m., the lobby and the theater were alive with displays, music, performers, and the conversations of a lively audience. Christine Ahn had invited a wide array of Bay Area groups—ranging from young male hip-hop fashion designers to Code Pink, a network of feminist peace activists. They were all crowded into the lobby, displaying their wares and talking with other attendees. Inside the theater, the show was about to begin. The lights went down, and the disc jockey started to spin her records. The master of ceremonies was a tall African American woman, herself a performance poet. She was soon joined by local rappers talking about war and peace. The stage began to fill with camo. There was camo casual wear, there were camo ball gowns.

Then there were "blasts from the past." One participant told the story of khaki—how khaki wasn't coined by the Gap but was an Afghan word to describe the distinctive color of that country's stark hillsides, which the British imperial army adopted for their own uniform colors but only after their red-coated troops were defeated in their initial efforts to subdue the region's less dramatically attired tribal fighters. Khaki as Americans know it has its roots in military conquest. The lights then focused on a well-known and longtime Bay Area Latina activist who strode to the front of the stage wearing a classic 1940s outfit—hat, gloves, brass-buttoned coat, and pumps—all in patriotic red, white, and blue. She was followed by a slender young woman wearing nothing but a bikini. The audience cheered. Then the poet MC told them that the bikini was created by a designer who wanted to exploit the international popular interest in the U.S. atomic bomb testing in the Pacific, which rendered Bikini, an island, uninhabitable. The audience uttered a collective gasp.

That was the goal of Christine Ahn and her WCRC colleagues. She didn't want to lecture these California women and men about what to think about the camo in their closets. She hoped instead that the fashion show would start them thinking and developing their own thoughts about militarization and about their own personal relationships to militarization.

Thousands of miles away, in Turkey, other local activists were organizing their own innovative event—one they hoped would raise ordinary civilians' consciousness about the dailyness of militarization and generate new awareness of that often invisible process.

They didn't choose a fashion show. These Turkish activists, women and men, many of them feminists and anticonscription activists, instead organized a militarism tour. They called their event "Militourism."

Taking people on bus and walking tours around Istanbul and Ankara, they pointed out buildings where every day some small or major strand of militarized Turkish life was woven. Most of these places were the sort that civilians passed every day without noticing and without thinking about what was going on inside, about what was being done there in their names, for their protection, for the "good of the nation." It is not as if Turkish women and men are unconscious of the central role that the military has played since the 1920s in shaping both public policy and national myths of unity, modernity, masculine duty, and the secular state. The Turkish military has made itself too prominent to be overlooked. Yet the organizers of the annual Militourism events wanted to make even clearer to their fellow citizens that both the military and practices of militarized living were more diverse and more "ordinary" than perhaps even the reader of the daily newspapers realized (Altinay 2004; Mater 2005).

In Israel, a small group of middle-aged Jewish women (and now several young women and men in their new youth group) have come together, one by one, and call themselves New Profile. Out of their concern that children's lives were becoming militarized, they tried to build bridges with Israeli academics involved in the country's educational system. It has turned out to be hard work. They also decided to take their messages about militarism into modest local sites. These women created a traveling exhibit to reveal how ideas about soldiering, about the country's recent past, about the military's centrality in Israeli life are even inserted into primary school children's education. The exhibit isn't flashy. It was assembled by the New Profile women themselves by looking at what their own children and grandchildren and nieces and nephews were being shown in schools and in contemporary children's books. They mounted their findings on five-foot-high folding boards. The women have to be able to carry these boards around the country, to Haifa and Tel Aviv, as well as to Jerusalem, and assemble the exhibit without fuss. A New Profile member sits by the exhibit wherever

119

they get permission to set it up—in schools, in local community centers, at conferences. She doesn't lecture the people who come to look at its images and captions but is there to answer any questions or just to engage in conversation. At first glance, some people who come think that the exhibit is in praise of the military. Only on closer inspection do they see the problematic relationships and ideas being revealed. There is a guest book, too, in which anyone who comes to look at the exhibit can share their own reactions. Underlying the New Profile modest exhibit is an ambitious goal: to inspire their fellow citizens, especially their fellow Jewish citizens (15 percent of Israel's citizens are non-Jews, mostly Palestinian Israelis), to weigh the costs of having created or consented to such a deeply militarized public culture.

A fashion show, a tour, a small display of children's books. These are not the usual activities for analyzing militarization or laying out the steps for demilitarization. But the San Francisco, Oakland, Istanbul, Ankara, Tel Aviv, and Haifa activists who created these events did so because they had become convinced that if militarization took myriad and often unnoticed forms, then demilitarization would start only when the invisible became visible, when the naturalized was made problematic.

Members of each group believed in the power of ideas—ideas about what is stylish, what is normal, what is educational. They believed that popularly held ideas—not just interests, policies, or institutions—were the source of militarization. Thus, all of these people working for demilitarization had become convinced that only through raising new questions in the minds of their fellow citizens could fresh conversations begin—conversations that might eventually turn into pressures for demilitarization.

Demilitarization. Today we are learning—often painfully, and usually reluctantly—that demilitarization may be one of the toughest transformative processes to carry through in all its steps to completion. To demilitarize any society—or even to demilitarize just a town, an organization, a television network, a family, a school, or a sense of yourself—turns out to require changes many of us would rather avoid. We want to don our camo shorts if they are deemed fashionable. We want to walk around our cities without questioning what is going on in their bland-looking buildings. We want to trust that our young children are learning healthy lessons in their schools. We want to keep cashing our paychecks from our employers, even if their executives bid on defense contracts. We want to hold our marriages together without scrutinizing our partner's work. We want to continue to be accepted as patriotic.

Many demilitarizing actions go unnoticed. They are taken by individuals without fanfare. But that lack of public attention doesn't necessarily make demilitarizing steps easy to take, particularly if militarism's beliefs, values, and practices have become normal or even glorified:

- A South Korean prodemocracy activist decides to critique how she and her fellow activists adopted militaristic ideas and strategies even as they sought to topple the country's military regime (Kwon 2000).
- An American young soldier decides to refuse to return for a second tour of duty to Iraq because he has come to see the military's actions there as unjust (Laufer 2006).
- A Chilean middle-aged woman buys new sneakers for her elderly mother and aunt so they can take part in antimilitary rallies and run away from the tear gas.
- A nineteen-year-old Jewish Israeli woman decides to resist her army conscription notice, even while most of her friends are accepting theirs, because, she explains, after volunteering for local groups seeking to support abused women, she now realizes that by becoming a soldier she would violate her principles as a feminist (Halili 2006).
- A Puerto Rican woman tells the story of how in the early 2000s she gained new self-confidence by mobilizing with her neighbors to force the U.S. Navy to withdraw from its military base and stop using her island of Vieques as a bombing range; her story is being circulated globally to women and men in Diego Garcia, Hawaii, Aruba, Guam, and other places with U.S. military bases (Lutz forthcoming; Ferguson and Mironesco forthcoming).
- An American mother and father together decide to sign the waiver, offered by their child's school in very small print on an official form, so that the name and home address of their son,

a high school senior, will not automatically be sent by school officials, along with all the other seniors' names and addresses, to the Pentagon recruiting command. They decide that would be an invasion of their own and their child's privacy.

- An Argentine mother decides that even though the military has been ousted from power, she will not give up pressuring the now-civilian elected government to bring the generals to justice (Arditti 1999).
- An American career diplomat, after deciding that a preemptive invasion of Iraq violates her profession's principles and after thus deciding to give up the career she loves and to resign from the U.S. Foreign Service, writes a letter to the secretary of state not claiming vague "personal reasons" but spelling out her principled objections to the government's policy.
- A Canadian woman living in Winnipeg, Manitoba, decides to speak out against Ottawa's plan to conduct urban warfare military maneuvers in her city.
- Yugoslav parents take great personal risks to get their son out of the country, to Germany, so that he won't be conscripted into the army, which the then Milošević-led government is deploying to Bosnia to pursue its Serbian nationalist goals.
- The father of an American Latino soldier who was killed in Iraq decides that he cannot grieve in private, that he needs to go to high schools with large Latino enrollments to speak to students about the reasons Latino young people should not enlist in the U.S. military.

Some of these individual actions remain just that. The person may be scorned or admired now and then by his or her family and colleagues, but otherwise few people pay any attention to that person's decision and the reasoning behind it. Occasionally, however, enough individuals discover that they are not alone in their thinking and actions, that they can create a group; perhaps, over time, enough small groups connect with each other that they together become a more sprawling network, a "movement."

On even fewer occasions news of such individual and collective decisions and actions can travel across national boundaries and start to globalize. This happened with the Mothers and Grandmothers of the Plaza de Mayo, a group of older women who stood up to the military in Argentina, insisting after the end of military rule that senior officers be held accountable for their abuses. News of their actions traveled to Turkey, where it inspired Turkish women to organize as mothers calling on the militarized government to provide news of their missing sons and daughters (Baydar and Ivegen 2006). This is similar to what has happened over the last century as individuals (mostly men) in many countries have resisted compulsory military service ("conscription" or "the draft"), have compared experiences, and often joined by women supporters who become integral to the movement, have created international networks of support for conscientious objectors.

Occasionally, a demilitarizing action will make the headlines. For example, on July 5, 2006, the U.S. Supreme Court, by a majority of 5–3, concluded that the president and his secretary of defense could not wave aside the Geneva Conventions and American judicial rules in order to try men held prisoner in Guantánamo in extrajudicial military proceedings. The case was *Hamdan v. Rumsfeld*, named for the plaintiff, a man held in Guantánamo without charges or a trial for over four years, and the secretary of defense. Commentators were surprised that the five justices in the majority did not do what judges often prefer to do, namely, justify their ruling on the narrowest possible grounds (leaving themselves plenty of room in future decisions). Instead, they went so far as to confirm the relevance to their judgment of the Geneva Conventions. No Guantánamo prisoners gained release as a result of the justices' decision, but *Hamdan v. Rumsfeld* was considered a landmark decision because it effectively challenged the executive branch's argument that these were "times of war" and that in "times of war" the American president can claim extraordinary authority (Greenhouse 2006). In this sense, the justices were trying to roll back the militarization of the U.S. political system at least a step or two.

Today feminists in many countries are showing us that trying to demilitarize anything requires making difficult changes in relationships between women and men—as well as changes in relationships between men and the state and between women and the state and even between women and women. Some efforts at demilitarization thus take place within the most intimate relationships—for instance, two people trying to reduce the secrecy that has come to riddle their relationship because one of the partners works on a weapons manufacturer's classified project. But other efforts to roll back militarization happen in the global arena.

Globalized demilitarization. Think of the 1997 international Mine Ban Treaty. Ultimately, this agreement was arrived at between governments. Yet those governments came together to hammer out the agreement and then (mostly) to sign its pledge to stop producing and using land mines because of the educational and political lobbying done by internationally minded nongovernmental activists. Jody Williams, a young Vermont woman, and the organization she founded, the International Campaign to Ban Landmines (ICBL), were awarded the prestigious Nobel Peace Prize in 1997 for the work they did around the world to convince government officials that landmines should be banned. They had witnessed and documented the devastating consequences of land mines for women, men, and children—most of them noncombatants (Stiehm 2006). A rural Cambodian or Mozambique child with an artificial leg became the global symbol of what land mines—which lie unmarked in deadly wait beneath the soil of a farmer's field or along a rural path years after the warring sides have signed peace agreements—can do.

The Mine Ban Treaty was signed in Ottawa in 1997. The Canadian foreign minister had taken the lead among government officials in the final stage of the international campaign to turn the grassroots effort into a multilateral agreement among governments (Beier 2004). Although one of its own citizens was awarded the Nobel Peace Prize for campaigning for the treaty, the U.S. government refused to sign or ratify it. Resistance from the Pentagon proved decisive. Defense officials argued—and members of the White House and the Senate (in the U.S. system treaties must be ratified by the Senate) agreed—that land mines were too valuable, for instance in separating North from South Korea, to be given up. The U.S. government has continued to refuse to sign or ratify the Mine Ban Treaty. Today there continues to be activist work going on to pressure the non-signing governments to sign the treaty and the signing governments to ensure that land mines are not produced or deployed. Feminists are involved, since they have found that even land mines are gendered: first, rural women and men in mined regions are affected in their daily lives differently because they play different roles in farming, traveling to markets, and making community decisions about who has the knowledge to plan any de-mining efforts; second, inside international aid groups it is often presumed that only men have the expertise to organize complex de-mining operations; and finally, within those governments that have refused to sign the anti-mine treaty, it is often deemed "soft" and "feminine" to object to the continued deployment of land mines.

There are a number of international—that is, government-to-government—agreements designed to limit the barbarity of warfare. They can be seen as efforts not to demilitarize the world but to globalize the ethics of militarized behavior. Most prominent among these globalizing efforts are

- the Geneva Conventions;
- the Convention against Torture and Other Cruel, Inhuman or Degrading Treatment or Punishment;
- the Mine Ban Treaty;
- the Convention on the Rights of the Child; and
- the Treaty of Rome, establishing the International Criminal Court (the world's first permanent "war crimes tribunal").

The effectiveness of each of these agreements depends on government officials actually signing *and* ratifying them. Signing is often politically easier for a government to do than ratifying, since by ratifying a treaty that government can be held internationally responsible for implementing its pledges. Even after a sufficient number of the world's governments have signed and ratified one of these agreements, its actual implementation and enforcement relies on the political commitment and will of government officials and attentive citizens (Reichberg, Syse, and Begby 2006).

How many high schools include the study of all of these agreements in their curricula? How many colleges require students to take courses that spell out the history and implementation of these agreements? How many law schools devote time to these legal commitments? Do many legislators consider it part of their political responsibility to challenge their governments to ratify them and then to enforce them? Do many local civic groups spend time becoming familiar with these agreements? When do voters weigh the appeal of a candidate on the basis of her or his stand on any of these treaties?

If the answer in any country is "not many," "almost never," or maybe a flippant "Are you kidding?" then it is worth asking a follow-up question: *why*? Could it be that such dismissive responses suggest that globalization is not as rampant as we usually presume? Globalization, in other words, seems to lose its momentum when what is being globalized are restraints on war waging. *That* is worth investigating.

Demilitarization calls for more than silencing the cannons. Those working for demilitarization with feminist analytical tools have discovered that ideas about manliness have to be addressed (Munn forthcoming; Conway forthcoming). For example, one of the most widespread programs that the United Nations introduces in societies that are trying to implement precarious peace accords is called Disarmament, Demobilization, and Reintegration, or "DDR" as post-conflict field workers routinely call it. Nowadays DDR is seen by its proponents as integral to international peacekeeping in countries around the world trying not just to bring wartime violence to an end but to lay the groundwork for a sustainable peace. DDR is a tough political assignment. When tried in Northern Ireland, El Salvador, East Timor, Congo, Liberia, Mozambique, Kosovo, it has met with resistance. People who have found safety, influence, and even a deep sense of identity in their possession of guns, sometimes walking and sleeping with those guns for years, are not likely to easily surrender them to international workers simply to garner what seem to be dubious offers of food, medical care, and training for new peacetime jobs. Guns have come to mean too much to those who hold them.

Conflict-zone officials and field workers until recently saw the gun holders to whom they were addressing their DDR appeals as just "soldiers" or "combatants" or "militiamen" or "insurgents." They didn't see them explicitly as men or as boys. It has taken interventions—not always welcomed—by feminists in nongovernmental organizations to expose what was missing in this conventional DDR approach: a questioning of masculinity. These soldiers, combatants, militiamen, and insurgents were not only those things but were men with anxieties about their reduced power in peacetime and pride in

126

their status as gun-holding masculinized men. Unless those ideas about—and needs for—masculinity were directly and effectively addressed, lasting disarmament, demobilization, and reintegration were not likely to be achieved. And thus demilitarization would be partial, superficial, and short lived (Farr and Gebre-Wold 2002; Farr 2006). Lepa Mladjenovic, one of the founders of the Belgrade Women in Black, is a longtime activist working to end violence against women. She explained to an audience in New York in 2005 how a decade after the signing of the Dayton Accords, the internationally brokered agreements intended to end the war in Bosnia, men's relationships to guns had changed in her city. As a volunteer in groups supporting women subjected to violence, she could see that over the past ten years of "peace" there had been an increase in men's use of guns and an increase in men's access to guns. As Lepa Mladjenovic explained to her American audience, "The gun is no longer in the cellar or the closet, it is now visible so that it can be used by the man in the home as an instrument of intimidation."

While too few of the planners and administrators of DDR have explicitly thought through what the politics of masculinity means for their actions, feminist activists and organizational workers have realized that most of these DDR planners and administrators do implicitly take for granted that DDR is about men and boys. That is, they have planned and carried out their programs as if all the people they will be dealing with in DDR camps would be men, although they avoid taking seriously in their operations the workings of ideas about manliness.

The reality in wars is more complicated. Feminist researchers working closely with local women's groups in conflict regions such as Uganda, Sierra Leone, Sri Lanka, Mozambique, and Liberia have had gender questions in the front of their minds. They have been wary of the vague term "child soldiers." The concept of the "child soldier"—and the reality it represents—has indeed aroused a new concern about children as young as eight being recruited, often forcibly, into armies. Nor have "child soldiers" been only those third world boys and girls who capture media attention because they are sent into conflict operations. The practice of turning children into soldiers, many activists contend, should include the more widely adopted and seemingly more benign government policy of authorizing, promoting, and funding voluntary school-age cadet corps (New Profile 2004).

A new public consciousness was created through global campaigning by the Coalition to Stop the Use of Child Soldiers. Founded in 1998 by Amnesty International, Human Rights Watch, the Quakers, the Jesuit Refugee Service, and several other organizations, the Coalition to Stop the Use of Child Soldiers helped mobilize international support for ratifying and implementing the UN Convention on the Rights of the Child, passed in 1989. By 1998, 117 governments had signed and ratified the historic convention (Singer 2006). Other governments, such as the British and the U.S. governments, have been reluctant to sign and ratify the convention because it might hamper their programs to introduce military cadet programs in high schools.

It is not that feminist-informed researchers and international peace workers criticize the use of the popular term "child soldier," they just don't think it is adequate. If one is committed to demilitarizing children who have been recruited into armies, then, they have found, one must ask when and how gender matters in how those children have experienced soldiering. So these feminist-informed researchers and practitioners have asked, "Where are the girls?" And following up on this innovative question, researchers discovered that girls have been recruited or coerced into fighting forces by all armed groups in a conflict and have been used by male commanders as porters, cooks, nurses, fighters, and sexual slaves (sometimes called "wives").

Moreover, these feminist researchers discovered that very few of these girls were receiving care from international or local organizations engaged in peacekeeping and national reconstruction. For instance, many of the agencies administering DDR camps made the handing in of a rifle the "ticket" for admission into the demobilization camps and the healthcare, job training, education, and psychological counseling those camps offered. But in most fighting forces, girls, while they played important roles in sustaining those forces, were only rarely issued guns. To make the DDR services accessible to girls trying to remake their lives after being used by fighting forces, the gun criterion would have to be eliminated. Furthermore, once one starts asking "Where are the girls?" one has to appropriate

128

a lot more funding for the sort of post-traumatic stress syndrome care designed for girls who have endured sexual abuse, a lot more resources for girls who, while still only sixteen or seventeen years old themselves, have come out of the fighting forces with small children of their own as a result of having been used as older male commanders' "wives." "Girl-headed household" would have to be a concept used by any policymaker who hoped to implement a realistic and meaningful postwar peacekeeping and reconstruction program (McKay and Mazurana 2004; Fox 2004; Krosch 2005).

In 2000, a first-of-its-kind international policy decision was made that is making it sound less "odd" and more "reasonable" to ask "What about masculinity?" and "Where are the girls?" In October 2000, delegates to the UN Security Council passed Resolution 1325. For the first time in its fifty-five years, the UN Security Council passed a resolution specifically addressing the condition of women. Resolution 1325 called on all UN agencies *and* the officials of all of the 184 UN member states to do two things they had neglected or resisted doing.

First, Security Council Resolution 1325 called on both staff members of all UN agencies, as well as officials of all UN member governments, to pay explicit attention to the conditions and experiences and needs of women in war zones. No longer, according to Resolution 1325, could rapes of women—by anyone—be swept under the rug or dismissed as merely a natural phenomenon of war. No longer could "refugees" be planned for and administered as if distributing food rations through men as alleged "heads of households" had the same political consequences as distributing those supplies through women. No longer could "child soldiers" be treated as if girls and boys in a fighting force had had the identical experiences—and thus had the same postconflict traumas or socioeconomic prospects.

Second, Resolution 1325 called on UN and government agencies to make sure that women, especially in local women's organizations, had a voice in decision making at every step of the peace process. No longer should the negotiations to craft the conditions for a ceasefire among the warring groups be an all-male affair. No longer should women be left out of the closed-door decision-making processes that constructed the new security forces, new legislature, new

executive, new constitutional provisions. No longer should international and local male officials and leaders feel satisfied when they
had considered women as mere victims. Under Resolution 1325,
women, including those victimized by the warring parties, should
be treated as political players.

Like the Mine Ban Treaty, the Geneva Conventions, the Convention against Torture, and the Convention on the Rights of the Child,
Security Council Resolution 1325 is an agreement ultimately voted
on by governments. Yet Resolution 1325 also owes its ideas to nongovernmental activists and its passage to the pressure applied by
those groups, who finally persuaded the governmental delegates to
pass it. In the story of the passage of Resolution 1325, the intellectual and strategic roles played by the women of the Women's International League for Peace and Freedom (WILPF) who worked in the
New York office across the street from the UN were crucial (Hill,
Aboitiz, and Poehlman-Doumbouya 2003; Hill, Cohn, and Enloe
2006).

Among the less anticipated consequences of the passage of—and
interpretation and attempted application of—Resolution 1325 has
been the shining of a bright light on the gender dynamics inside the
international peacekeeping operations themselves. When more people began to take seriously the experiences, ideas, and organizational priorities of women and women's organizations in societies to
which the United Nations and NATO were sending peacekeeping
and reconstruction teams, they began to ask fresh questions about
whether the international civilian aid providers and military peacekeepers themselves might be having a less-than-positive impact on
local women's and girls' lives. This meant taking stock of the masculinized and racialized biases among "the good guys." Many people
used to seeing themselves as the rational, well-meaning, civilized,
altruistic actors were, not surprisingly, uncomfortable under this
new scrutiny.

"Peacekeepers" suddenly could be seen as men—men with particular, often diverse notions of what it meant to be deployed as a
soldier on a peacekeeping mission. That is, their own notions of
masculinity were revealed as a significant factor in how they conducted their militarized peacekeeping operations. Women and girls
in Cambodia, East Timor, Bosnia, Kosovo, and Liberia would have

to figure out ways to cope with—and organize and strategize to confront—those notions and the men's behaviors that flowed from them. And local women in societies coming out of militarized conflict would have to confront men in international peacekeeping forces at the same time as they sought to challenge abusive behavior and arrogance of men in their own communities—men who often acted out their own sense of frustration, anger, and confusion with violence toward women in their households, communities, and refugee camps (Joshi 2005; Cockburn and Zarkov 2002).

When international aid workers, peacekeeping officials, and government and private foundation donors assumed that reaching out to "local leaders" meant working with the men who had influential positions in the postconflict societies—leaders of villages, town mayors, heads of political parties, clerical authorities—then the patriarchal hurdles that local women activists confronted in trying to have a voice in peacemaking and national reconstruction loomed even higher: those male "local leaders" were often no less scornful of women's policy ideas than the international officials reaching out to them. That is, "local leaders," when left ungendered, is not in itself a guarantee of the sort of representation that can move a society effectively toward sustainable demilitarization.

Many male soldiers chosen by their home governments for deployment on UN or NATO peacekeeping missions still attach the highest value to combat. The appeal of combat is why they joined the military. Combat experience is what would earn them the greatest respect (and maybe promotion and extra pay) from their military comrades and superiors and from their fellow citizens back home. Combat is what they had been trained for. Combat would earn them the sought-after status of "real men" (Whitworth 2004).

Further undermining many peacekeeping soldiers' ability to engage in effective peace building are their stereotypes about the women and the men in the country to which they are deployed—the women as needing their superior protection, the men as not being capable of protecting their women. They exchange needed food for a "date," not thinking of it as having anything to do with prostitution, but feeling that they, the manly men, are doing a good deed (Higate and Henry 2004).

Because serious consideration about the interplay of demilitariz-

131

ing policies and the politics of militarized masculinity was not "on the agenda" prior to the passage of Resolution 1325 and only barely given the nod after the formal passage of Resolution 1325, peacekeeping has been experienced by many women as prostitution, sex trafficking, and sexual harassment (Refugees International 2005).

So much of this new global feminist-informed thinking about demilitarization—what it is, what undermines it, how it can be achieved and sustained—hinges on revising our ideas about *security*. Security turns out to be a broad, many-layered goal. It can no longer be imagined as simply synonymous with militarized security. Security, many women activists working to end armed conflict in various countries have concluded, has to be seen more realistically and more broadly, and that means it has to be seen as more complicated (Jacobson 2005). Security is one of the goals of demilitarization because so many people have discovered that militarization—that is, coming to see the world as dangerous, learning to be preoccupied with enemies, bolstering executive power in the name of fighting those enemies, starting to define one's patriotism and the criteria for belonging according to military service, or deferring to those who have done military service—has caused them to feel less, not more, secure. Security for many women and girls also comes, more are beginning to realize, less from fortifying the country's borders or driving out of their towns people of other ethnic groups than from finding ways to escape violent assaults perpetrated by men in their own homes.

Yet the familiar militarized ways of conceptualizing security remain stubbornly entrenched.

Listen to Nadine Puechguirbal. She is a French woman with years of experience on UN peacekeeping missions in Congo and Haiti. Her recent job was as "gender advisor" to the UN peacekeeping mission in Haiti, a post created by the UN to carry out its new responsibilities under Resolution 1325. Nadine Puechguirbal discovered, though, that neither the international military nor the police units deployed to bring peace to the Haitian people—a people who had endured years of dictatorship, partisan gang warfare, and a succession of devastating hurricanes and floods—were ready to expand their conventional ideas about creating security. Nor did these experts want to take seriously the ideas of the local Haitian feminists—women whom she had found to be practical, knowledgeable, and committed.

She summarized the typical reply of those male peacekeeping military officers who resisted her attempts to bring these Haitian women activists to the planning table: "They don't need to participate in the decision-making process because we can do this for them." And if this familiar assertion that women are merely victims, not decision makers, seemed wobbly, then the international officials fell back on claims of urgency: "It's an emergency, we have no time for gender, we'll add that later." The results?

- Women became the recipients of the internationally distributed food, but only the distribution points were staffed with peacekeepers, and on the long walks home, over the hills, women were attacked by armed male gangs who stole their precious supplies.
- International administrators of Haiti's new elections thought of security in conventional terms, deploying military peacekeepers only around the polling stations, without considering the more realistic ways in which Haitian women strategized about security; thus when election day came, many women did not walk the miles to the nearest polling station both because they could not trust that their children would be safe while they were away for hours and because they realistically feared they would be attacked on the long walk to vote (Puechguirbal 2003, 2006).

While the U.S. government voted for Resolution 1325 (it is a resolution, not a treaty, and thus does not require signing and ratification), the resolution—its analytical premises, its requirements—is virtually unknown among Americans. Neither U.S. officials nor any reporters covering American military or civilian policies and practices in Afghanistan or Iraq ever mention Resolution 1325. That does not mean that some Afghan women haven't heard about Resolution 1325. One of the strategies of the WILPF and other supporters of the ground-breaking Security Council resolution was to distribute the text of Resolution 1325 to as many local women's groups around the world as possible—that is, to globalize Resolution 1325 in order to give local activists a sense of empowerment and to provide them with a lever to open up the still-masculinized political processes in their own war-torn or postconflict societies.

In Afghanistan one of the principal critiques articulated by local Afghan women's groups is that the U.S. occupying forces and their superiors in Washington depended heavily on the male commanders of the regional militias (referred to as the Northern Alliance) in their military invasion to topple the Taliban regime, without taking into account how militarized and patriarchal those commanders were. Consequently, now, with the new constitutional system's legislature and president (and his cabinet) struggling to exert their civilian authority, those conservative militarized commanders (often called "warlords") remain entrenched in positions of power as governors, police chiefs, and the dominant bloc in the newly elected legislature. One member of the new legislature, Malai Joya, a twenty-seven-year-old woman already active in a local women's organization, won a seat in the 2005 national elections. What made her famous among Afghans was her standing up in the new legislature in December 2005 to denounce those male legislators who were "criminal warlords . . . whose hands are stained with the blood of the people" (Coghan 2006; Coleman and Hunt 2006). In the wake of her public denunciation of the patriarchal and militarized warlords, principal players in the anti-Taliban Northern Alliance, Malai Joya was subjected to death threats.

What Malai Joya underscored in her dramatic speech was what Resolution 1325 also implies: demilitarization cannot be achieved unless women are empowered to the point that all the forms of masculinized militarization are exposed and rolled back. Most of those local and international officials determining how peace building and postconflict reconstruction will proceed do not think in these terms. In their planning for the U.S.-led invasion and occupation of Afghanistan, American officials did not think deeply about the causes of militarization or about what it would take to reverse it; they made forming alliances with the existing anti-Taliban warlords a priority. The ramifications of that U.S. decision continue to be felt in the lives of Afghan women and men (Enloe 2004).

In Sweden, the government has provided funds for the Swedish branch of the WILPF to conduct a Resolution 1325 education program in Swedish schools, raising both teachers' and children's awareness of the new reasoning about security, peace, and gender that undergirds the passage of 1325 and the responsibilities now on the shoulders of Swedish soldiers when they are deployed on UN peacekeeping missions abroad. One WILPF staff woman tells of going into a school and getting a discussion going among the young students about how certain sorts of ideas about what it means to be a man or a boy can undermine peace and security. One boy, she remembers, joined in with this candid admission: he does sometimes try to act "macho" and even physically threatening when girls are around, just to impress them. Other boys in the class laughed and rolled their eyes. But the first boy held his ground: "You know that you do this too!" The others didn't deny it. That was exactly the sort of open discussion about gender, peace, and security that the WILPF women hoped to inspire by bringing Resolution 1325 into everyday Swedish life.

Similarly, Israeli Palestinian and Jewish feminist activists working together in Haifa, Israel, have decided to "bring 1325 home." They have looked carefully at all the provisions of Resolution 1325 and found that many of them should be applicable to both the Israeli-Palestinian conflict and the everyday relationships between women and security forces inside Israel itself. Gendered assumptions and practices, these Haifa feminist activists reveal, have to be explored at the same time as the ways ethnicized and racialized notions and behaviors are candidly explored and questioned (Aharoni and Deeb 2005).

Demilitarization efforts in so many countries—both developed and developing, both war-torn and war-waging—have been resisted by those individuals and groups who have realized—even if they do not say it out loud—that pushing a demilitarization process beyond tokenism would require dismantling patriarchal structures, not only in the public realm, but in the private sphere as well. Genuine, lasting, and thoroughgoing demilitarization, in other words, would have to alter the relationships between women and women, between women and men, between men and men, and between women and men and all the influential institutions of society—schools, legislatures, religious organizations, corporations, the media, the military, the offices of prime ministers and presidents.

Successful demilitarization calls for changing the relationships between masculine authority figures and feminized "dependents," awarding the education department as much political influence as the defense department, and withdrawing from male citizens—especially those claiming insider military knowledge—their privileged status as the citizens presumed to be "expert" on security issues.

7

THE DIVERSE LIVES OF MILITARIZED AND DEMILITARIZED WOMEN: GLOBALIZING INSIGHTS FROM LOCAL JAPANESE PLACES

Militarization is a step-by-step process. *Demilitarization* is also a many-step process. None of the steps in either militarization or its reversal, demilitarization, is automatic. So every step has to be explained, its causes have to be spelled out.

We still don't fully understand exactly how and why militarization—or its reversal—"works." But we have learned that if we watch it as a process—something that happens to real people in big and little steps over time—we are likely to be more subtle. If we can be more subtle, we'll be more realistic in our explanations of militarization. If we are more realistic in how we explain militarization, then our recommendations for how to reverse it will be more effective. In other words, to be realistic, one needs to be subtle. To be *subtly* realistic—that's our analytical goal. To get there we will need to be curious about how militarization happens, not just to men, not just to governments or soldiers, not just to companies or political parties or universities, but to diverse women in their everyday ("unimportant," "trivial," "private") lives.

In this spirit of careful, subtle inquiry, it is valuable to look and listen to Japanese women today.

The constitution of Japan, written in 1947 under the U.S. postwar occupation authority, includes an article that is rare among the world's constitutions. Most Japanese simply refer to it as "Article 9." It reads: "Aspiring sincerely to an international peace based on justice and order, the Japanese people forever renounce war as a sovereign right of the nation and the threat or use of force as means of settling international disputes."

In order to guarantee this, Article 9's writers continued: "Land, sea and air forces as well as other war potential, will never be maintained. The right of belligerency of the state will not be recognized" (Fellowship of Reconciliation 2005).

The American government, using its occupation authority during the late 1940s, pressured the Japanese to include this innovative article in their postwar constitution. Nevertheless, within less than a decade many American officials had begun to exert pressure on their Japanese counterparts to commit themselves to diluting Article 9.

Once the horrors of World War II had faded and had become replaced in Washington by anxieties over the tensions of the U.S.-USSR globalized rivalry, American officials looked to Japan to serve as an ally—as a militarized ally—against both the Soviet Union and China, each defined as Communist threats to U.S. national security. Beginning in 1950 and still today, U.S. officials of both political parties have pressured the Japanese government to create a formidable modernized military, to allow the U.S. to base naval, marine, and air force offensive units on its soil, to contribute Japanese taxpayers' yen to maintaining those U.S. bases, to participate in joint military maneuvers in Asia, and more recently to contribute military forces, albeit in carefully defined "noncombat" roles, to the U.S. military occupation of Iraq (Johnson 2003).

Some American officials have intimated that only a fully remilitarized Japan would be a Japan worthy of taking a seat as a permanent member of the UN Security Council because only a militarized industrial power is a genuinely "mature" global player. Such an assumption might be seen as the militarization of international maturity—and of the UN Security Council.

Today, Article 9 still stands, but many Japanese fear for its survival. For these worried Japanese, most of whom have grown up since World War II, Article 9 is central to their understanding of what it means to be Japanese in a globalized world. Article 9's pledge guarantees that Japan will play its international roles economically, politically, and culturally without relying on military might, thus making Japan a country that has the potential for developing broad global respect and trust.

For other Japanese, however, Article 9 is imagined to be the embodiment of humiliation. To them, it is a reminder of Japan's wartime defeat, surrender, and transformation at the hands of foreign occupiers. Article 9, in their eyes, hamstrings their country's ability to play the influential international leadership role it should, given its impressive economic achievements at home and abroad. A country that has created Sony, Mitsubishi, Honda, and Toyota, they believe, should be able to possess unfettered military might to complement those corporate giants. These promilitarization Japanese remain a minority but are growing in numbers and in political and popular influence. They argue that a "normal" country is one equipped with a full-fledged military and a pride in its own history. They applaud the government's recent decision to move the Self Defense Forces director out from under the prime minister's office and to a cabinet office of his own. They call for public singing of the national anthem in schools and at public events and showing the red-sun flag in schools and public places, practices until recently frowned upon by most Japanese. They want to require antimilitarist teachers to use textbooks that play down the Imperial Japanese Army's atrocities in World War II. They tend to support the right wing of the long-ruling electoral party, the Liberal Democratic Party. Thus, as in most countries, the debates about the costs and rewards of choosing militarization over demilitarization get played out in the arena of political party contests (Onishi 2006).

If they feel passionately about the need to eliminate Article 9, some Japanese may support the most outspoken nationalists, the men with bullhorns who shout their nationalist slogans outside Tokyo's busy shopping centers and subway stations. These vocal nationalists call on their compatriots first, to "get over" their collective guilt from World War II and second, to support the buildup of the country's military power in order to confront the forces of North

Korea and China. They brush aside the anxieties expressed by their other Asian neighbors, many of whom still remember the horrors of occupation by the imperial Japanese forces in the 1930s and 1940s (Onishi 2006).

For many Japanese today, however, Article 9 remains a source of pride and security. They see this innovative constitutional provision as evidence that Japan will not revert to its earlier ways, which they interpret as having been imperial, colonizing, nationalist, and militaristic. They prefer to see the defeat in World War II as the source of important lessons—lessons that, if learned, will allow Japan to play a leading role globally as a model of how a country and its people can pursue prosperity without relying on authoritarianism and militarization. These Japanese worry about the apparent present-day marriage of convenience between the emerging Japanese nationalist, militarizing political right wing on the one side and on the other, those in Washington pressuring Japan to remilitarize.

Among these critics of Japanese remilitarization are Japanese feminists. While conservative nationalists have argued that guilt over past wars is debilitating and that building and deploying a military force is the avenue for taking Japan's rightful place in global affairs, Japanese feminists have been pursuing quite a different path toward globalized participation. After having launched new historical research, they are now acknowledging their uncomfortable finding: during the 1930s and early 1940s many ordinary Japanese women embraced a militarized version of nationalism, actively supporting their government's wars, as housewives, mothers, wives of soldiers, city workers, farmers, and community organizers (Ueno 2004). This acknowledgment hasn't been easy.

Hundreds of Japanese women activists traveled to take part in the UN-sponsored international meetings marking the Decade of Women (1975–1985); even more Japanese women attended the historic UN-sponsored Beijing Conference on Women in 1995; and at least four hundred Japanese women—more than from any other country—traveled to New York in 2000 to take part in the "Beijing Plus Five" UN conference called to monitor the implementation of the Beijing Platform for Action signed by scores of governments in 1995, pledging them each to take steps to empower women. In addition, many Japanese women have been working in development aid projects from Uganda to Afghanistan and participating in dozens of smaller efforts organized with women from other Asian countries. With these actions, Japanese women's advocates have presented to their fellow citizens an alternative model of globalization—an alternative based on the argument that building trust through cooperation among equals holds out a better prospect for ensuring security than does nationalism-fueled militarization (Chan-Tiberghien 2004; Ueno 2004).

In December 2000, Japanese feminists active in a group called Violence Against Women Worldwide Network (VAWW NET) organized an international conference in the form of a women's tribunal to hear testimonies of women from around Asia—Korea, China, the Philippines, Taiwan, Indonesia, Singapore—who had been coerced during World War II into sexually servicing the male soldiers of the Imperial Japanese Army. They had several goals. First, they wanted to shine direct light on their own government's and their fellow citizens' untenable denial of this wartime sexual slavery practiced in their name. Second, they wanted to build new alliances of trust and cooperation with women's advocates in other Asian countries—alliances that had continued to be hampered by many Asians' painful memories of previous Japanese conquest and imperialism. Europeans and North Americans often lump together women of such diverse countries as North and South Korea, China, Japan, Vietnam, Taiwan, Cambodia, Laos, Indonesia, Thailand, the Philippines, and Burma (renamed "Myanmar" by the military dictatorship) as merely "Asian." But being seen by Westerners as "Asian women" does not in reality guarantee shared memories, common understandings, or identical goals. Even launching a new journal published in Korea and titling it the *Asian Journal of Women's Studies* was subject to debate among the feminist scholars at the journal's home campus, Ehwa Women's University. After all, who was "Asian"? Were there any significant shared experiences and identities among Burmese, Japanese, and Korean women?

The VAWW NET's 2000 tribunal, therefore, was both risky and innovative. It drew scores of participants and provoked new awareness and fresh conversations about what happened during World War II and what sweeping away the denials of those events might do to turn a new page in relations among women of the region. But the organizers were dismayed when, under pressure from conservative government officials, NHK, the major Japanese television network, backed down from showing a documentary film about the tribunal. For many Japanese feminists this provided another piece of evidence of the growing influence of militarizing nationalists in their country's political life. On the other hand, they were heartened that they were offered support in challenging NHK by a trans-Asian feminist coalition called the Asia Pacific Forum on Women, Law and Development, which is based in Thailand. Its support suggested that the VAWW NET activists' second goal, to build new relationships of trust between Japanese feminists and women's advocates throughout Asia, was coming within reach (Kashiwazaki 2006).

The debate going on among Japanese today—and the significant role of the United States in influencing that debate, as well as the stakes the people of China, Taiwan, Indonesia, and Korea have in the outcomes of this debate—makes it crucial that we understand the diverse ways in which Japanese women experience militarization and resistance to militarization. Moreover, the debates that Japanese women are engaging in today resonate in many countries. Japanese women and men are not alone in being encouraged

- to interpret their country's constitution in ways that make it easier for the executive branch to deploy the military;
- to teach children that the country's past is unblemished; and
- to define a "normal country" as one with a potent military force.

I had the chance to visit Okinawa in March 2003. Okinawa once was an independent kingdom but was conquered by Japan. It was as a province of Japan that Okinawa was invaded by the large U.S. military force in 1945 as part of a strategy for defeating the Japanese and ending World War II. The March to June 1945 Battle of Okinawa was one of the most devastating battles of the war. For the next thirty years, the U.S. government ruled as the occupying authority in Okinawa, even after the rest of Japan was returned to sovereignty. These were the years of the Cold War. American military strategists came to value Okinawa as a major military base. Many of its marines and pilots deployed to Vietnam were stationed in Okinawa. In 1972, under pressure from a reviving Japan, the United States returned

Okinawa to Japanese rule, but with the important proviso that the United States would be allowed to continue to use hundreds of acres of valuable farm and coastal lands in Okinawa for its military bases. In fact, two-thirds of all the thousands of U.S. troops now stationed in Japan are stationed on its small southern island, Okinawa. This arrangement between the two governments has inspired neither trust nor gratitude among many Okinawans toward officials in Tokyo or their counterparts in Washington (Taira 2003). On the other hand, most Americans would have a hard time finding Okinawa on a world map, much less describing its complex political place in global militarized politics. Thus, my own brief visit to Okinawa in 2003 was a chance to be tutored.

There were five of us from mainland Japan (I was then a visiting professor in Tokyo) who were hosted by Suzuyo Takazato and other Okinawan women active in the group Okinawa Women Act Against Military Violence (OWAAMV). The visit was eye-opening for me.

On the last day Kaori Hirouchi was seeing off a mainland Japanese colleague, Amane Funabashi, and me at Okinawa's main airport. Kaori brought her little seven-month-old baby with her to the airport. When she saw me, she exclaimed, "Look at what a friend just gave me!" As women always do for their friends with new babies, several of Kaori's friends had passed along used baby clothes. The exchange of used baby clothes is one of those economies only a feminist might notice. Kaori said, "Look at this." She pulled out a pair of cute little baby socks. Her friend in Okinawa had given her these socks because they would fit her new little son beautifully. The miniature cotton socks were khaki and were decorated with images of little bomber airplanes. Standing there in the airport, Kaori holding the baby socks in her hand as one would a piece of valuable evidence, the three of us began wondering together: What did her friend think of as "cute"? Can one militarize "cuteness"? Can one militarize the friendships between women as mothers?

Our feminist curiosities were sparking now. Would her generous friend have thought it appropriate to pass along to Kaori these same hand-me-down bomber-decorated socks if her baby were a girl? Does living as a woman in Okinawa, where the operations of U.S. military bases weave in and out of civilian daily life, make bombers seem as ordinary or as "cute" as a toy fire truck or a panda bear?

Baby socks. If we activate our feminist curiosity, we can plumb deeper into the subtleties of feminized militarization—how and why motherhood can (never automatically) become militarized; how the most seemingly harmless of fashions can (again, never automatically) become militarized; how friendship between women can sometimes become militarized. Baby socks? Lacking a feminist curiosity, baby socks will appear trivial—that is, not worth paying attention to in one's search for causes. It requires an active feminist curiosity to treat these seemingly "nonpolitical" events with analytical seriousness, to understand their causal potency.

On our first day in Okinawa, we mainlanders were taken around the main island by Keiko Itokazu, a woman who had become an active member of OWAAMV and, more recently, an elected member of the Okinawa prefecture legislature. She took us to World War II memorials, to museums, to the famous caves. And as we drove in the car from place to place, Keiko Itokazu pointed out open fields and fenced-off areas, telling us their political histories. Keiko Itokazu describes her profession as that of a "peace guide." Suddenly, I realized, "Oh, all the other guides are *not*." But Keiko Itokazu hadn't always been a "peace guide." That is a profession she has helped create on Okinawa. She began her career in Okinawa's "second industry," tourism, as a tour-bus guide. Up in front of the bus, microphone in hand, Keiko would give visiting tourists, most of them sunseekers from chilly mainland Japan, the conventional rendition of Okinawan history, offering her listeners a historical vision of heroism and sacrifice during the horrific Battle of Okinawa. Over the miles in between these featured sites, she would give her voice a rest, finding little of interest to talk about as the rural Okinawan landscape passed by.

Several years ago, however, a group of Okinawan peace activists invited the local tour-bus guides to meet for a conversation. It was a challenging conversation. The peace activists asked Keiko and her fellow guides: "Do you realize that in the way you're practicing your own profession you are helping to militarize memories—Okinawans' memories, tourists' memories? Do you realize that by saying nothing about lost arable land, about what all these miles of fences mean, you are militarizing every visitor's understanding of the landscape and making the conversion of vegetable farms into military runways seem normal?" The peace activists pressed each of their fellow Okinawans working as tour-bus guides to assign more serious meaning to their seemingly "trivial" occupation, to see for the first time the deep implications of what they said up in the front of their tour buses—and what each chose to leave unsaid.

Not all of the tour guides who participated in this uncomfortable conversation decided to transform their profession—to take steps to demilitarize tour guiding. But Keiko Itokazu did. She could only *de*-militarize her profession, however, if she, working with women in OWAAMV, could figure out what exactly was militarized in her previous script and what was militarized in her previous silences.

This might be a good point at which to remind ourselves what it means for a person, an occupation, a relationship, a town, an industry, or a memory to become militarized. First, anything is on its way to becoming militarized if it is increasingly coming under the control of a military—of a military's rules, its budget, its command structure. Second, and perhaps harder to chart, anything is becoming militarized if it is increasingly (more than last year, more than a generation ago) dependent on militaristic ideas, concepts, or values for its safety, its sense of self-worth, its status of belonging, its economic well-being, its social legitimacy, even its alleged "normalcy." As we have seen, women and men do not become militarized in identical ways. Furthermore, almost anything—a town, a school, a company, a museum, a legislature, a ministry—becomes militarized in significant part due to someone's manipulations of ideas about femininity and ideas about masculinity.

Now let's look at what it takes today for a particular Japanese woman to resist these subtle everyday workings of militarization. We have to travel to Kyushu, one of Japan's three major islands, south of Tokyo, but north of Okinawa. When I visited Kyushu, it was February. The mud was soggy and the air cold. Only a few brave plum trees so far had dared to bloom. A former graduate student and now a globally minded feminist, Yukiko Oda, introduced me to Hiroko Watanabe. Yukiko Oda and I spent an afternoon and evening with Hiroko Watanabe, learning how she had become committed not only to resisting her own militarization but also to making visible the minute ways in which her Kyushu neighbors were being sucked, step by step, into the process of militarization. Hiroko Watanabe is a dairy farmer. Dressed in blue jeans and muddy sneakers, her hair cut short, Hiroko exudes a sense of purpose—actually, a sense of multiple interlocking purposes. Hiroko is determined to sustain her small dairy business, an occupation that she believes provides life-giving food, despite the ups and downs of government and industry pricing.

At the same time, Hiroko Watanabe is determined not to surrender to the pressures on her to become passively resigned to the expansion of the Japan Self-Defense Forces (SDF) base in her town of Tsuiki. She walks us around the fenced perimeter of the SDF base. She points out the F-16 fighter planes parked on the runway. She makes sure we look at the decorative bushes at our elbows, planted just outside the base fence and paid for by the SDF—as a gesture of "neighborliness." Or is it an effort at cooptation? You can militarize a dairy farmer. You can militarize a flowering bush. She shows us the main gate to the base where on the second day of every month, for over a decade now, Hiroko Watanabe and anyone else who is moved to join her come to sit with banners calling for respect for Article 9 of Japan's "peace" constitution.

Hiroko Watanabe gets up at five o'clock every morning. From six to ten, she milks her cows and cleans out their stalls. From five to nine every night, Hiroko does her second four-hour shift, returning to the barn to milk the other half of her cow herd and clean out their stalls. Cows are tyrants. If you are a dairy farmer, you cannot ever leave your cows. So resisting your own militarization and the militarization of your fellow townspeople has to be done in the few hours between your shifts with the cows.

Over tea in her home, Hiroko tells Yukiko Oda and me of the constant pressures on citizens of Tsuiki and of the three other towns whose land the SDF now controls: pressures to accept Tokyo money, pressures to accept Tokyo-designed construction projects, pressures to hand over more land for air force runways, and pressures to give up any sense that their elected diet and local council representatives can shape military policy. When the men in these elected posts speak of the SDF's impact on their towns, they speak, Hiroko explains, in the tones of "rationality." To be rational, after all, is to be masculine. To be masculine is to be rational. Even a woman trying to break into the masculinized world of Japanese electoral politics must adopt this "rational" stance if she wants to be taken seriously in the masculinized halls of government. But what if this sort of masculinized rationality is really only a camouflaged version of political resignation? What if this "rationality" is a means for elected officials to accept the imposed militarization without appearing helpless and thus feminized?

Hiroko Watanabe has refused to measure her own rationality in these masculinized terms. Instead, she—in between her daily morning and evening milkings and barn cleanings—publishes a newsletter to make visible the typically ignored minutiae of local militarization. In doing so, in refusing to adopt a masculinized form of resignation, Hiroko of course risks being labeled "unrealistic" and "naïve"—"feminine."

Baby socks. Motherhood. Friendship. Tourism. Bus guides. Memory. Farmland. Construction projects. Femininity. Town councilors. Rationality. Masculinity. Civilian resignation.

The things that seem to need to be militarized for the sake of implementing and legitimizing a militarized national security policy are far more numerous and diverse—and often far from the inner sanctum of political elites—than we usually imagine. And the workings of gender together with the lives of women weave in and out of every one of them.

Only by exercising a feminist curiosity—only by taking seriously the exploration of women's daily experiences and often trivialized ideas—are we likely to discover the appropriate explanatory weight that each of these deserves. While femininity is almost always manipulated (rewarded, nurtured, taught, discouraged, punished, avoided) in the process of militarizing national security, femininity comes in more than one form. There are, we are realizing thanks to all the cross-cultural, cross-class, cross-generational women's studies investigations, myriad femininities. Thus, to realistically explore how the processes of gendering militarization both rely on and serve to shape ideas and practices of both masculinity and femininity, we will have to keep our curiosity open to diverse femininities being militarized separately but often simultaneously.

Take, for instance, an imagined woman we will call "Angelina." She is a white American woman in her mid-thirties married to an officer in the marines who is still in the early stages of his military career. He has just been assigned to a U.S. base in Okinawa. Angelina is nervous about being so far away from her family and friends in her home state of Florida. But she is relieved that she has at least been able to go with her husband to this Okinawa posting. She's been so lonely when he's been deployed overseas for months at a time. Angelina is just getting settled on the base in Okinawa and is pleased because the military family apartment she has been assigned at Camp Foster is so much better than the housing that she and her husband had on the military base back in North Carolina. She's heard from other marines' wives that this is because these U.S. base apartments are paid for by the Tokyo government. Plus, she thinks there are such great recreation facilities on this base for her two children. So here is Angelina living in Okinawa as an American military wife. She is far away from friends and has given up the chance to have a career of her own. But for now, she reasons, there are at least the warm breezes of Okinawa and the marine housing facilities at Camp Foster to enjoy.

At the same time, to the north in Tokyo, an imagined Japanese woman, "Yoko," is busy strategizing about her own career in what she has come to see as the thoroughly masculinized world of Japanese international journalism. Yoko is in her late twenties. She does not want to be a decorative feminine presence serving as an anchor on the evening news. Instead, Yoko wants to be sent overseas to cover real news. She wants to break into the men's world of foreign correspondents. It's early 2003, there is a war looming in the Middle East. Yoko has persuaded her senior editor to let her join the team from a major national newspaper, the *Asahi Shimbun*, that is being sent to cover the probable U.S. invasion of Iraq. This is a breakthrough. Yoko will be the first woman reporter in the history of the *Asahi Shimbun* assigned by this still-male-dominated prestigious newspaper to cover a war. Yoko is not a warmonger. She is personally opposed to the government's Liberal Democratic Party–controlled cabinet's support of the Bush administration's war policy. But, she thinks to herself, this war may offer her a great career opportunity. War is where so many male journalists have made their reputations. So Yoko is packing her bag; she is on her way to Iraq.

She will prove to her editor, to her male colleagues, and to the Japanese newspaper readers that a woman can do a "man's job"—cover a war.

Now let's turn our attention again to the south, back to Okinawa. But this time let's pay serious attention to the life and thoughts of a woman we will call "Mrs. Miyagi." She defines her own femininity largely in terms of being a good wife. Her husband is a fisherman who fishes off the coast just north of Naha City. This is where Tokyo government officials and Washington government officials have agreed that the U.S. base further south will be relocated; the existing military base, Camp Schwab, will be expanded so that it can accommodate the military plane U.S. designers have named the "Osprey." Japanese officials thus approached Mrs. Miyagi's husband and pressured him to sell his fishing rights to the government so that it will be easier to consolidate this land for the military base without much local opposition from the people in and near Naha City. Mrs. Miyagi and her husband talked about it together. It was a big decision. They decided that there wasn't much choice; Camp Schwab was going to be expanded one way or another. Of the two, her husband was more resigned; he thought taking the Tokyo/Washington money was the most rational thing to do. But Mrs. Miyagi was hesitant. She had women friends in the coastal towns who were hanging banners, selling vegetables to raise funds, doing everything possible to stop the Camp Schwab expansion into their ecologically valuable bay. If she agreed with her husband to sell his fishing rights to the government, would she be letting down her friends?

Already we can see that there is not just one kind of femininity that is being militarized. The U.S.-fostered and the locally encouraged militarization of Japan require the militarizing transformations of the ideas, hopes, aspirations, fears, and work of diverse women—most of them Japanese. But some of those women who need to be militarized in order to ensure the militarization of Japan are American women.

Femininities are intersected with class, ethnic, generational, and national dynamics. Yet in each instance, it is a form of femininity that is being militarized. If we are *not* curious about the complex workings of femininity in particular women's lives, we will not be able to reliably explain why and how the subtle process of militarization occurs—or is reversed.

Also, as even just these three examples reveal, a variety of femininities are being manipulated to fuel militarization in not just one but several countries simultaneously. So today, in order to realistically explore efforts to remilitarize Japan, we need to look outside Japan, to the United States. Let's think about a woman we'll call "Cheryl." She is an African American woman, nineteen years old, and she has joined the U.S. Navy right out of high school because she has heard from both her older brother and her Chicago high school guidance counselor that you are less likely to experience racism in the U.S. military than in most American civilian workplaces. Furthermore, the navy recruiter tells Cheryl that, once she has enlisted, the navy will help her pay for a future college education. She is determined, somehow, to go to college. She is also aware that the U.S. economy is unpredictable; so many of her friends are having a hard time getting more than a minimum-wage job. So, overall, even though she doesn't imagine a world populated by enemies and knows that security takes forms that have little to do with submarines and rockets, Cheryl decides that joining the navy makes sense.

After finishing basic training, Cheryl is pleased when she is assigned to a supply ship that is soon due to sail to Yokohama. Her mother is worried. She has heard Washington officials sounding so eager to "wage war on terrorists." Cheryl's mother believes that if her government spent more on education and community-styled policing, there would be less crime and more security in her own Chicago neighborhood. But Cheryl assures her mother that serving on a supply ship, she will not be anywhere near combat; even if she is deployed to Iraq, she will be offshore, not patrolling roads through insurgent neighborhoods. Moreover, Cheryl tells her still-skeptical mother, African Americans are more likely to gain full equality in American society if they prove that they are patriotic. And what is more patriotic than joining the U.S. Navy? Cheryl is one of the American sailors now living in Yokohama.

Consider now another American woman, "Susan." Her life is also about to become tied to the lives of Japanese women. She is a white, precariously middle-class woman living and selling real estate in a small city in upper New York State. She is in her fifties, divorced, and a single mother with two teenage sons. The younger boy is doing fine. He loves school, has an after-school job, and helps Susan with the laundry. But Susan worries about her older son, Tom. He's been out of high school for almost a year. He just squeaked through to graduate. Now he hangs around the house all day, drinking Cokes, watching television, and playing war games on his computer. Susan feels she has failed as a mother. Maybe if Tom joined the marines, it would make a mature man out of her son. With this hope in mind, she decides to give him motherly encouragement when he shows signs of enthusiasm after seeing the enticing recruiting ads for the marines on television. If her son succeeds as a soldier, Susan thinks, she could feel like a successful mother. She worries about her son being deployed to Iraq, so she breathes a sigh of relief when Tom is sent to Okinawa. Neither Susan nor Tom has ever heard of Okinawa, but when they look on a map they can see it is far away from the Middle East.

I had been trying out some of these ideas about how particular women thought about their own relationships to the military during a series of evening talks in Tokyo. I wondered what members of the audience thought. So during the evening I asked them—women and men—to do some of their own imagining and to stand up and "become" a woman whose femininity has been (willingly or unwillingly) militarized for the sake of perpetuating—or maybe questioning—the U.S.-Japan government-to-government international security alliance. There were lots of volunteers.

"I am a Filipino woman working near a U.S. military base in Okinawa," the first woman explained. She explained that (in this guise) she had immigrated to Japan by paying a hefty fee to an employment agency. She also explained that she grew up on one of the poorer islands of the Philippines and hoped to work as a respectable entertainer with a migrant worker's visa issued by the Japanese government. But now she found herself in Okinawa. Back home in the Philippines she had prepared for work abroad by learning a full repertoire of American rock 'n' roll and country and western songs. But now here in Okinawa she wasn't singing; she was working in a disco, trying to persuade male customers to buy her diluted "ladies' drinks" and supplying sexual services to young, bored American male marines in the decaying discos just outside the gates of Camp

Hansen. She is afraid to tell her parents. Her mother is sure to be disappointed, seeing her as failing to live up to the standards of a respectable Catholic Filipino woman. Furthermore, she is barely making enough money to send home to her rural parents. Now that the yen-dollar exchange rate has left the American men with little spending money, some of her customers prefer the cheaper system of bringing women to their living quarters inside the base, thus avoiding the disco-owners' bar charges. Although this practice is allegedly a violation of the U.S. Marines rules, no American officers seem to pay much attention when their soldiers bring civilian women onto the base for sex.

A man in the audience stands. "I am a female employee of a Japanese construction company. I work as a secretary," he explains. "I'm forty-five years old. I could only find this part-time job. But it really helps cover the family's expenses because my husband's own full-time job with a big bank is so insecure. Some of his friends already have lost their corporate jobs. I know that the Liberal Democratic Party (LDP) legislators and the national government tell local town councils that the government will build new roads, bridges, even sports centers, in return for the town's cooperation in voting to host an SDF or U.S. military base. I'm not sure that this is a good trade for the local people. But we've had a decade of recession here in Japan and in this still-fragile economy, I need to keep my clerical job. So I'm really relieved that my boss has developed such close relations with the ruling LDP and gets some of these lucrative construction contracts in the military-base towns. These government contracts make my own job a bit more secure. My girlfriends and I are going to Hawaii on vacation next month."

A woman then stands. "I am a girl who has recently gotten a job as a civilian employee inside the U.S. Navy base at Yokohama because I want to be able to buy jeans cheaper and eat American food." This member of the audience is in her fifties, but she is trying to think like a twenty-one-year-old Japanese woman. She knows how seductive U.S. consumer culture is for many Japanese. "I can shop at the PX on the base and can eat at the McDonald's on the base for much less than at the McDonald's in Ikebukuro." Neither the cosmetics sold at a discount in the PX nor the "Chicken McNuggets" at McDonald's seem to this young Japanese woman to be remotely related to war, to foreign policy, or to violence. Furthermore, in her bookkeeping job on the base, she can improve her English: "Everyone knows that to get ahead today you need to be able to speak English. For a Japanese woman, I think that is especially valuable, don't you?"

It is worth pausing here for a moment to take an accounting of what has been militarized as a result of militarizing these women's—Japanese, Filipino, and American—feminized lives tied to Japan: daughterhood, marriage, motherhood, secretarial and bookkeeping jobs, learning English, fast food, education, patriotism, entertainment, sexuality, consumerism, economic security, and fashion. Militarizing femininities—in all their diversity—seems to be crucial for sustaining the Tokyo-Washington bilateral military security agreement. If one pays no attention to the politics of femininity in particular women's lives, it is likely that any commentator on international politics will end up with an unreliable analysis of the politics that today perpetuate the Japanese-U.S. alliance. This does *not* mean that women control the alliance. They clearly have little power in alliance negotiations. But the male elites of both countries do rely upon a lot of women to think of their own feminized lives in ways that make militarization "normal" and thus almost invisible.

Now back to the audience. "I am an Okinawan woman who has trained as an actress," a woman in the back row tells us. "I have just gotten the chance I've been working for: I have been invited by a major Japanese film director to audition for a film set during World War II. I will play the female romantic lead, the fiancée of a brave Japanese pilot." She then explains that she knows from her mother and her Okinawan teachers that the Battle of Okinawa was not just a story of romance and bravery and that many Okinawans of her grandparents' generation paid a terrible price for being caught in the middle between the imperial and American forces in the spring of 1945. "But the film script is wonderful. And how often does an Okinawan actress get a chance to play the romantic lead in a mainland-produced film? I have to try out for it. And, after all, it's only a love story!"

At this point in our discussion, I wondered aloud what members of the audience thought were the reasons increasing numbers of young Japanese women were volunteering for the Japan Self-Defense Forces. Did their motivations have to do with the politics of femininity in contemporary Japan? As Japanese professor Fumika Sato has uncovered in her important research, Japanese civilian officials in charge of SDF planning, motivated by a desire to expand the country's military without diluting its quality, have raised women's proportion of the SDF's soldiers to 4 percent, an all-time high. But that 4 percent has been achieved only because many young women now have their own reasons for enlisting in the SDF.

At this point three women—of different ages—suddenly stood up. The first woman, in her sixties, imagined herself as a member of the SDF and playing that role, told us: "I am single and twenty-six years old. I majored in mathematics at university and also in graduate school. I wanted to work for the SDF as an air traffic controller because it's a field that requires mathematical skills but is not open to young women at civilian airports." This contribution showed us that the militarization of a woman-as-mathematician is easier in a society that presumes that mathematics is a "naturally" masculinized profession. If this same Japanese twenty-six-year-old were male, therefore, he would have more opportunities open to him in the civilian air traffic controller profession, and thus it would be harder to militarize him. By contrast, the officials making personnel decisions for the SDF categorize "combat" jobs as the most masculine and thus today might tolerate some dilution of the masculinized culture in other job sectors of their military, for instance, in their own air force control towers.

Not all women who volunteer for the SDF, however, are motivated by identical aspirations. A second woman, also role-playing, explained: "I had just graduated from high school and was looking for a job. I saw a recruiting poster—all the people looked nice, they were smiling, there were no guns, and I thought the uniform was cool." This contribution makes us look again at the militarization of women's fashion. Fashion designers are always thinking about varieties of femininity. Some fashion designers work for militaries. Militaries all over the world think about the design of their uniforms so that they can appeal to men's sense of masculinity and to women's sense of femininity. Military officials debate about uniforms, especially where to put the pockets. There are government memos about where to place military women's pockets: they have to be functional and militarized, yet feminine. That can be a tricky formula to fulfill.

"I have applied for the SDF because the women entering the SDF can live on the base," a third woman who is imagining herself as an SDF woman volunteer began. "If I don't have to pay for housing, I can save money. My plan is to stay inside the SDF for three or four years. Then, with the money I save, I will do postgraduate studies in Tokyo, get a professional certificate, and have an independent civilian career. So I see joining the SDF now merely as a means to an end. I'm not joining the SDF just to look for a husband, as I hear some other young women do. And I'm not interested in being a soldier. Honestly, I'm even a bit worried about the fact that the government is now sending war ships and peacekeeping units overseas to the Middle East. Doesn't that violate Article 9? Well, I don't know much about politics. I just want to use the SDF as my own stepping-stone to an independent woman's life. I'll let the politicians worry about the big questions."

After hearing all these imagined women's voices, a woman toward the back stood up with determination. "I'm going to be myself. I'm for Article 9. I know what it means. That's one of the reasons I decided to join Tokyo's Women in Black. Well, 'join' isn't exactly what you do with Women in Black. It's a very loose and non-hierarchical group. We don't hold meetings or elect officers or pay dues or give speeches. Maybe you've heard of the Belgrade and the Jerusalem Women in Black groups. They've been nominated for the Nobel Peace Prize for the antiwar work they do in their countries. Here in Tokyo, any woman can just come and join our Friday evening vigils in Shinjuku. You can't miss us; we're the little circle of women with shoppers swirling around us. Some of the Friday night shoppers do pause to read our signs, and if they ask us questions, we do answer. Most of us try to come wearing something black. Any woman is welcome to join the circle. I see here in the audience tonight several women who come regularly. We stand silently at the bottom of the long outdoor subway escalator, in the glow of those huge neon signs. We keep our messages simple. We just hold up homemade signs saying 'Women against Violence' or 'No to War.' Last Friday some women wanted to make the links between peace and antiracism, so they brought along their own small signs that said 'Support the rights of Koreans in Japan.' After our hour's vigil, we usually go to a nearby Italian restaurant to have a bite of supper and get to know each other. Yes, Japanese peace activism, feminism, and Italian pasta can all go together!"

Few of the women and men who stood up to speak of women's varied experiences of joining in militarization—or challenging it—used the term "globalization." Yet almost all of them spoke of their own globalized consciousness. That is, each of these Japanese audience members who shared their ideas that evening implied that even a woman living what seemed to be quite an apolitical and parochial life was thinking and acting within a web of international relationships.

Each participant there in the Tokyo auditorium also revealed how a militarizing process relies on the manipulation of diverse women's sense of their own femininity. In other words, militarization in any society (both in wartime and in alleged "peacetime") can be pushed forward only if diverse women's own beliefs about what it means to be "feminine" can be manipulated or exploited. Moreover, militarization—in Japan, but also in the United States, Britain, China, Russia, Israel, Argentina, Sudan—requires that the ideas about women's "femininity" held by women's and girls' families, employers, teachers, boyfriends, husbands, and political leaders be made to fit militarizing forms. As always, the politics of femininity is a tree with many branches and meandering subterranean roots.

What I learned from my Japanese friends and colleagues was that we will be able to fully and accurately explain how and why militarization happens—or why sometimes it is stalled or reversed—only when we sharpen our feminist curiosity, when we investigate the pressures shaping women's lives as well as women's own ideas about their work, their identities, their worries, their desires.

Yet this sort of investigation is still often dismissed as not "real" politics. So it seems as though changing what counts as "real" politics is going to be a necessary part of getting a more realistic—and reliable—grip on the causes and consequences of local and global militarization.

CONCLUSION: THE GLOBAL, THE LOCAL, AND THE PERSONAL

The year 2005 was a good year for global arms sellers. According to the highly respected independent weapons monitoring group, the Stockholm International Peace Research Institute (SIPRI), during 2005 the world's total military expenditures reached a stunning all-time high of $1.1 trillion. To make the statistic easier to grasp, that amounted to spending, in just one year, $173 on militaries for every single woman, child, and man on the planet. Of course, not every government was spending equal amounts on their militaries. Mexico's military expenditures may be higher than many of its citizens wish, but those expenditures won't be in the same league as, say, the expenditures of Jordan or France. The global distribution of expenditures among the world's almost two hundred governments is indeed strikingly lopsided: during the post–Cold War decade 1996–2005, military expenditures of the United States alone accounted for "almost half of the world total" (Stockholm International Peace Research Institute 2006, 15).

Jet fighters, armored vehicles, missiles, and heavy artillery aren't cheap. A lot of governments were spending large slices of their resource pie to act out their militarized vision of "national security." Among the national governments spending the most on their militaries are those of Britain, France, Japan, and China. In 2005, they each accounted for 4–5 percent of the world's total military expenditure. These proportions are significant and raise the eyebrows of many British, French, Japanese, and Chinese citizens, who wonder whether these public funds might be better spent on other projects that would enhance their fellow citizens' security. But these proportions still pale next to the Americans' 48 percent of the world's military expenditure total (Stockholm International Peace Research Institute 2006, 15).

A lot of this government spending is for arms bought and sold internationally. The weaponry market has indeed become globalized. That is, not only Nike, Sony, BMW, and Dunlop are globally marketing their products and encouraging potential consumers to develop needs and desires they may not have thought they had. So too are manufacturers of heavy and light weapons. Most of their customers are governments. Usually, government officials from the manufacturer's home country see themselves as commercial enablers: they perceive their own public responsibility as one of helping their country's manufacturers win sales of their weapons abroad. Playing this role—and, more deeply, perceiving this as among their public duties—serves to militarize many trade, commerce, and industry department officials.

Once again, militarization happens to many more people than just those in uniform or those who work in defense ministries or national security agencies. It can happen to an engineer or to a physicist pursuing a corporate career. It can happen to a treasury or finance official worried about the country's imbalance of imports and exports. It can happen to a commerce or industry official whose performance will be judged on the basis of whether she or he succeeds in "opening markets" for local arms manufacturers.

Furthermore, the sorts of companies now competing for defense contracts are more diverse than ever. A generation ago it was chiefly the makers of arms and high-tech weapons that were throwing their corporate hats into the defense-contracting ring. Nowadays it is construction companies, advertising companies, and providers of food services, health services, banking services, telephone services, entertainment services, and intelligence services. The person offering this caveat is the director of SIPRI. At a seminar held in Stockholm recently, Alyson Bailes, herself a career British diplomat before becoming the head of SIPRI, warned other attendees not to complacently imagine that women are positioned in the economy so that they are less likely to be militarized. She noted that a lot more women today who are making their way up the corporate ladder will likely face decisions about whether it is good—or risky—for their own companies to join the competition for government defense contracts.

That is, there always have been women militarized within the traditional (and still powerful) defense contractors—women as secretaries, women in the personnel departments, women on the factory floor doing wiring, a handful of women in engineering, plus all of the women married to defense contractors' male engineers, computer programmers, physicists, accountants, lobbyists, and senior executives. Nevertheless, these companies—for example, Lockheed Martin, Boeing, Raytheon, Saab, Rolls-Royce—have been deeply masculinized in their corporate leadership and their organizational cultures, making women's militarization seem less likely or at least less obvious. By contrast, some of the companies newer to defense-contracting competition have been somewhat less masculinized; that is, these have been companies in which more women have been able to rise through the professional and managerial ranks.

As government defense officials multiply the products and services that they privatize—that they farm out to private, civilian companies—more and more women with MBAs seeking to use their skills and talents in the world of private business will be prone to militarization. No longer will women executives be somewhat less subject to direct militarization simply because they are not working for companies that produce rifles, night-vision goggles, body armor, missiles, and submarines. These women executives—trying to gain markets for their food products, telephone services, magazines, computer games, housing services—also will be more likely to have to decide whether their firms should depend for any part of their profits on serving military goals.

This serves as a warning: militarization—at home, nationally, and globally—has to be tracked over a long time. A short attention span can lead the tracker to flawed explanations. Flawed explanations generate flawed prescriptions.

The changes in defense contracting suggest another caveat: to track militarization one will need to monitor changing gender patterns within diverse organizations, as well as the pressures on those trying to graduate from outsider to insider status within those competitive worlds.

As we have seen, militarization is a process that binds together the personal, the local, the national, and the global. Look at college students in Massachusetts who have chosen to major in engineering. How will they—and their parents and professors—react to the following recent newspaper article? "Prodded by state government officials fearful of alienating a key Massachusetts industry, nine Bay State colleges and universities have agreed to adapt their engineering curriculums, and in some cases introduce new courses, to meet the needs of defense contractors" (Weisman 2006).

The reporter goes on to describe how the Massachusetts state governor and his economic development aides are worried that if Massachusetts colleges do not train students in the sorts of skills desired by locally based, globally competing defense contractors—for example, Raytheon and Lockheed Martin—those companies might lose future U.S. and overseas defense bids, which in turn, would damage the state's entire economy. This calculation suggests that already the state's economy has become significantly militarized; that is, it has become dependent not only on companies whose profits come from defense work, but on the principal source of defense monies, the military.

How did the presidents, deans, and faculty of Massachusetts colleges respond to the industry's call? Worcester Polytechnic Institute (WPI), the University of Massachusetts, Wentworth Institute of Technology, Northeastern University, Boston University, and Cape Cod Community College accepted defense-contracting companies' invitation to discuss the companies' curricular needs, such as new courses in defense-contract management and radio frequency engineering (Weisman 2006). If three years from now a young man or woman at WPI or Northeastern decides to follow an advisor's suggestion and take a course in radio frequency engineering, will he or she be aware of the militarizing process he or she is joining? Perhaps the young man or woman will be aware. Perhaps militarization will look to the student like the path to a well-paying and secure career, as well as a way to contribute to his or her country's national security and a healthy balance of import and export payments.

So militarization can appear attractive. It can be personally re-warding materially and emotionally. It can seem to make sense and be practical and efficient. Militarization can seem to be a reasonable response to a threat-filled, unpredictable world. In fact, the more convinced any person becomes of globalized or localized danger, the more likely he or she is to see the prioritization of military needs and militaristic values over other needs and values as positive, or at least inevitable.

This makes it necessary to explore ideas. Ideas matter. The idea that the world is a dangerous place is the seed of many militarizing processes. Alternative ideas portray the world as full of human cre-ativity, of the potential for human cooperation, or of opportunities for empathy and mutual respect. The many efforts taking place now—in Turkey, Afghanistan, Norway, Nepal, the United States, Sweden, Israel, Congo, Iran, India, Liberia, Haiti, Britain, South Korea, Serbia, Japan—to demilitarize societies are attempts to alter deep-seated, widely held ideas:

- ideas about threats
- ideas about protectors
- ideas about citizenship
- ideas about modernity
- ideas about history
- ideas about rationality
- ideas about security
- ideas about violence
- ideas about trust

Each of these ideas is fraught with blatant and subtle presump-tions about masculinity and femininity. Ideas about both masculin-ity and femininity matter. This makes a feminist curiosity a necessity for the careful tracker of militarization—both global and local. Equipped with a feminist curiosity, the tracker is most likely to always ask about the politics of masculinity and of femininity: Who benefits from which notions of masculinity? Who has the re-sources to make their presumptions about femininity the basis for foreign policy? And how do particular men and women living in places as different as North Carolina, Tokyo, and Baghdad live with the consequences of those gender-fueled policies?

For example, as we have seen, ideas about "security" can be interpreted so that they assign government priority to the government's military, which in turn tends to put the mostly male national security elite in positions of exceptional authority. On the other hand, "security" could be interpreted to mean what it takes for women as well as men to feel safe inside their own homes and neighborhoods or in refugee camps. This alternative interpretation of "security" would accord less authority to military experts and more authority to local women's groups whose activists have been collecting information about women's daily lives and devising ways to prevent rape and domestic violence.

Similarly, one needs to keep a sharp feminist eye on ideas about "protectors." Are the most effective protectors thought to be those trained to wield weaponry? If so, then again this interpretation is likely to make soldiers—and those with the authority to deploy them—seem to be the most dependable protectors. Since in most countries today soldiers are 85–100 percent male, women are cast into the position of the protected. Protectors, in turn, are imagined to be the "action figures" in civic life—those who not only can move (they are not tied down by domestic responsibilities) but can, it is frequently imagined, think rationally about which moves are most needed now and which moves can be shoved down the priority agenda until "later." Once more, the gendered interpretation of any one of these ideas will have implications for gendered thinking about other ideas on this list.

Ideas, however, don't just float out there in the ether. Ideas gain legitimacy and influence—or are quashed and discredited—within particular social settings: classrooms, television studios and newsrooms, Land Rovers and Humvees, legislatures, interrogation cells, behind-closed-doors strategy sessions, business meetings, courtrooms, banter-filled locker rooms, and dinner tables. These all can be sites in which to listen for the making and unmaking of those ideas about masculinity and about femininity that will move militarization forward—or roll it back.

And institutions and organizations, like ideas, are riddled with presumptions about and practices of femininity and masculinity. For example, within a given organization, what sort of person is deemed rational enough to make the "Big Decisions"? What sorts of labor are considered "unskilled" and are thus low paid? What are the group's collective assumptions about the kinds of people who can be trusted to keep secrets? Who is turned to as the group's "expert"? What sorts of people are thought to be "emotional"? The answers to these questions will determine whose ideas about "security" will hold sway as the organization goes about its day-to-day business. The answers to these questions also will determine which uses of violence are known to the public and which are kept secret.

Ideas don't gain primacy and become "normal" at the snap of the fingers. It takes time and many steps—most of them hardly visible, many of them seemingly trivial—for "national security" to become militarized, for soldiers to become the chief protectors, for a woman to become a "military wife," for an abuser to become merely a lone "bad apple," for men to become ashamed of any suggestion that they are "feminine." For this reason, tracking militarization—the interplay of ideas and social relationships over time—calls upon the tracker to "think big" and "think small" simultaneously. The astute tracker of militarization thus will listen for the jokes, read the daily memos, chart what is not said. At the same time, the tracker of militarization will put the pieces together in order to gradually map the larger patterns—the landscape, the doctrine, the culture, the climate, the system. Jokes *and* the culture, memos *and* the system, silences *and* the climate, apples *and* the barrel.

When gendered militarization becomes globalized, it works its way through ideas on the wings of institutions and organizations. This means that in order for us to track the many paths by which militarization travels, we need to stay deeply interested in the personal and the local and the national, while we also widen our lens to watch how those militarizing ideas, organizations, and processes move across territorial borders.

The tracker of globalizing militarization will thus develop a feminist curiosity about the workings of alliances, humanitarian organizations, international agencies, international media, international trade, the international movement of people as immigrants, soldiers, refugees, and diplomats.

Yes, the analytical order is getting taller and taller. But being realistic about today's globalizing militarization—how and why it happens, what its consequences are—is not a modest goal.

Those who have come to the conclusion that demilitarization is an honorable and valuable objective will need to develop the same tracking skills. The pursuer of demilitarization will need to make sense of how militarization occurs in the lives of individuals and families, in companies, in institutions, in nations, and across national borders.

There are steps being taken toward demilitarization—by students who ask that the history of peace movements be taught in ordinary history or political science courses, by parents who rethink what it means for a son to "become a man," by computer companies that decide to eschew defense contracts, by women's groups that pressure foreign aid managers to redefine "security," by activists and diplomats who help create new treaties and institutions to outlaw land mines, torture, child soldiers, ethnic cleansing, and wartime rape. Which steps are only temporary and soon undone? Which ones last? What are the implications of each of these steps for women? For men?

Tracking militarization and fostering demilitarization will call for cooperative investigations, multiple skills, and the appreciation of diverse perspectives. Simultaneous attention to the personal, the local, the national, and the global can't be done alone.

REFERENCES

Aharoni, Sarai, and Rula Deeb. 2005. *Where Are All the Women? UN Security Council Resolution 1325: Gender Perspectives of the Israeli-Palestinian Conflict.* Haifa, Israel: Isha L'Isha–Haifa Feminist Center and Kayan Feminist Organization.

Altinay, Ayse Gul. 2004. *The Myth of the Military Nation: Militarism, Gender, and Education in Turkey.* New York: Palgrave Macmillan.

Alva, Donna. 2006. *Unofficial Ambassadors: American Military Families and the Cold War, 1945–1965.* New York: New York University Press.

Alvarez, Lizette. 2006. "Military Fails Some Widows Over Benefits." *New York Times,* June 27.

Amnesty International, International Action Network on Small Arms, and Oxfam International. 2006. *The Impact of Guns on Women's Lives.* Control Arms. http://www.controlarms.org.documents/small-arms-women-report-final2-1.pdf.

Arditti, Rita. 1999. *Searching for Life: The Grandmothers of the Plaza de Mayo and the Disappeared Children of Argentina.* Berkeley: University of California Press.

Associated Press. 2006. "Dog Handler Convicted in Abu Ghraib Abuse." *New York Times,* June 2.

Barkawi, Tarak. 2006. *Globalization and War.* Lanham, MD: Rowman & Littlefield.

Basch, Linda. 2005. "Human Security, Globalization, and Feminist Visions." *Peace Review* 16 (1): 5–12.

Baydar, Gülsüm, and Berfin Ivegen. 2006. "Territories, Identities, and Thresholds: The Saturday Mothers Phenomenon in Istanbul." *Signs* 31 (3): 689–716.

Bauer, Jan, and Anissa Helie. 2006. *Documenting Women's Rights Violations by Non-State Actors: Activist Strategies for Muslim Countries*. Montreal: Rights and Democracy.

Beier, Marshall. 2004. "'Emailed Applications Are Preferred': Ethical Practices in Mine Action and the Idea of Global Civil Society." In *The Future of Humanitarian Mine Action*, ed. Kristian Berg Harpviken, 19–32. New York: Palgrave Macmillan.

Bowers, Simon. 2004. "Merrill Lynch Accused of 'Institutional Sexism.'" *Guardian* (London), June 12.

Broder, John M., David S. Cloud, John Kifner, Carolyn Marshall, Eric Schmitt, and Thom Shanker. 2006. "Contradictions Cloud Inquiry into 24 Iraqi Deaths." *New York Times*, June 17.

Brownfield-Stein, Chava. 2006. "An Army That Has a State? The Role of Israel's Security Establishment in a Comparative Perspective," Paper presented at the Van Leer Institute, Jerusalem, Israel, June 5.

Bunster-Burotto, Ximena. 1985. "Surviving Beyond Fear: Women and Torture in Latin America." In *Women and Change in Latin America*, ed. June Nash and Helen Safa, 297–325. South Hadley, MA: Bergin & Garvey.

Burke, Carol. 2004. *Camp All-American, Hanoi Jane, and the High-and-Tight*. Boston: Beacon Press.

———. 2006. "One of the Boys." *Women's Review of Books* 23 (2): 3–5.

Burns, John F. 2006. "Getting Used to War as Hell." *New York Times*, June 4.

Caraway, Teri L. Forthcoming. *Assembling Women: The Feminization of Global Manufacturing*. Ithaca: Cornell University Press.

Carver, Terrell. 2003. "Gender/Feminism/IR." *International Studies Review* 5 (2): 288–290.

Chan-Tiberghien, Jennifer. 2004. *Gender and Human Rights in Japan*. Stanford, CA: Stanford University Press.

Cloud, David S. 2006. "Inquiry Suggests Marines Excised Files on Killings." *New York Times*, August 18.

Cock, Jacklyn. 1995. "Forging a New Army out of Old Enemies: Women in the South African Military." In "Rethinking Women's Peace Studies," special issue, *Women's Studies Quarterly* 23 (3–4): 97–111.

Cockburn, Cynthia. Forthcoming. *From Where We Stand: War, Women's Activism, and Feminist Analysis*. London: Zed Books.

Cockburn, Cynthia, and Dubravka Zarkov, eds. 2002. *The Postwar Moment: Militaries, Masculinities, and International Peacekeeping*. London: Lawrence & Wishart.

Coghan, Tom. 2006. "Afghan MP Says She Will Not Be Silenced." Reprinted in *Women Living Under Muslim Law Newsletter* 18 (April): 4.

Cohn, Carol. 1987. "Sex and Death in the Rational World of Defense Intellectuals." *Signs* 12 (4): 687–718.

Cohn, Carol, with Felicity Hill and Sara Ruddick. 2005. *The Relevance of Gender for Eliminating Weapons of Mass Destruction*. Stockholm: Weapons of Mass Destruction Commission.

Coleman, Isobel, and Swanee Hunt. 2006. "Afghanistan Should Make Room for Its Female Leaders." *Christian Science Monitor*, April 24.

Conway, Daniel. Forthcoming. "The Masculine State in Crisis: State Response to War Resistance in Apartheid South Africa." In "Hegemonic Masculinities in International Politics," ed. Juanita Elias, special issue, *Men and Masculinities*.

Danner, Mark, ed. 2004. *Torture and Truth: America, Abu Ghraib, and the War on Terror*. New York: New York Review of Books.

Domosh, Mona. 2006. *American Commodities in an Age of Empire*. New York: Routledge.

Eager, Paige Whaley. 2004. *Global Population Policy: From Population Control to Reproductive Rights*. Aldershot, UK: Ashgate Publishers.

Ehrenreich, Barbara. 2004. "All Together Now." Op-Ed, *New York Times*, July 15.

Elias, Juanita, ed. Forthcoming. "Hegemonic Masculinities in International Politics." Special issue, *Men and Masculinities*.

Enloe, Cynthia. 1980. *Ethnic Soldiers: State Security in Divided Societies*. London: Penguin.

———. 1993. *The Morning After: Sexual Politics at the End of the Cold War*. Berkeley: University of California Press.

———. 2000. *Maneuvers: The International Politics of Militarizing Women's Lives*. Berkeley: University of California Press.

———. 2004. *The Curious Feminist: Searching for Women in a New Age of Empire*. Berkeley: University of California Press.

Eran-Jona, Meytal. 2005. "The Sailor's Girl: Gender Regime and the Militarization of Military Wives in the IDF." Research paper, Department of Sociology, Tel Aviv University.

Farr, Vanessa. 2006. "Gender Analysis as a Tool for Multilateral Negotiators in the Small Arms Context." In *Disarmament as Humanitarian Action*, ed. John Borrie and Vanessa Martin Randin, 109–136. Geneva: United Nations Institute for Disarmament Research.

Farr, Vanessa A., and Kiflemiriam Gebre-Wold, eds. 2002. *Gender Perspectives on Small Arms and Light Weapons.* Brief 24. Bonn, Germany: Bonn International Center for Conversion, July.

Fellowship of Reconciliation. 2005. "Petition to Support Article 9 of the Japanese Constitution." Amsterdam: Fellowship of Reconciliation.

Ferguson, Kathy, and Monique Mironesco, eds. Forthcoming. *Gender and Globalization in Asia and the Pacific.* Honolulu: University of Hawaii Press.

Filkins, Dexter. 2006. "In Shadows, Armed Groups Propel Iraq Toward Chaos." *New York Times,* May 24.

Fox, Mary-Jane. 2004. "Girl Soldiers." *Security Dialogue* 35 (4) 465–480.

Frühstück, Sabine. Forthcoming. *Uneasy Warriors: Gender, Memory, and Popular Culture in the Japanese Army.* Berkeley: University of California Press.

Giles, Wenona, Malathi de Alwis, Edith Klein, and Neluka Silva, eds. 2003. *Feminists Under Fire: Exchanges Across War Zones.* Toronto: Between the Lines.

Gillan, Audrey. 2005. "The Great Gurkha Race." *Guardian* (London), June 12.

Golden, Tim. 2006. "The Battle for Guantanamo." *New York Times Magazine,* September 17, 60–71, 140–145.

Goldenberg, Suzanne. 2006. "Woman Soldier Refuses Return to Iraq, Claiming Sexual Harassment." *Guardian* (London), June 21.

Greenberg, Karen, and Joshua Dratel, eds. 2005. *The Torture Papers: The Road to Abu Ghraib.* New York: Cambridge University Press.

Greenhouse, Linda. 2006. "Supreme Court Blocks Guantanamo Tribunals." *New York Times,* July 6.

Halili, Idan. 2006. "Interview with Feminist Refusnik Idan Halili," Tel Aviv, Quaker Service.

Hansen, Lene, and Louise Olsson, eds. 2004. "Gender and Security." Special issue, *Security Dialogue* 35 (4).

Harrison, Deborah. 2002. *The First Casualty: Violence Against Women in Canadian Military Communities.* Toronto: James Lorimer & Co.

Harrison, Deborah, and Lucie Laliberte. 1994. *No Life Like It: Military Wives in Canada.* Toronto: James Lorimer & Co.

Hartmann, Betsy. 1995. *Reproductive Rights and Wrongs: The Global Politics of Population Control and Contraceptive Choice,* rev. ed. Boston: South End Press.

Hawkesworth, Mary. 2006. *Globalization and Feminist Activism.* Lanham, MD: Rowman & Littlefield.

Henry, Monica K. 2006. "'Good Military Wives' Stay 'In the Closet': Obstacles to Openly Opposing Operation Iraq Freedom (OIF)." Unpublished master's thesis, San Jose, Costa Rica, Gender and Peacebuilding Program, UN University for Peace.

168

Hersh, Seymour M. 2004. *Chain of Command: The Road to Abu Ghraib.* New York: HarperCollins.

Higate, Paul, and Marsha Henry. 2004. "Gender in Peace Support Operations." In "Gender and Security," ed. Lene Hansen and Louise Olsson, special issue, *Security Dialogue* 35 (4): 481–498.

Hill, Felicity, Mikele Aboitiz, and Sara Poehlman-Doumbouya. 2003. " Nongovernmental Organizations' Roles in the Buildup and Implementation of Security Council Resolution 1325." *Signs* 28 (4): 1255–1270.

Hill, Felicity, Carol Cohn, and Cynthia Enloe. 2006. "U.N. Security Council Resolution 1325 Three Years On: Gender, Security, and Organizational Change." Boston: Boston Consortium on Gender, Security, and Human Rights.

Hillman, Elizabeth Lutes. 2005. *Defending America: Military Culture and the Cold War Court-Martial.* Princeton: Princeton University Press.

Hindustan Times. 2006. "Women on Top in Peace Force." June 6.

Holmquist, Caroline. 2005. *Private Security Companies: The Case for Regulation.* Stockholm: Stockholm International Peace Research Institute.

Hoogensen, Gunhild, and Kirsti Stuvoy. 2006. "Gender Resistance and Human Security." *Security Dialogue* 37 (2): 207–228.

Hooper, Charlotte. 2001. *Manly States: Masculinities, International Relations, and Gender Politics.* New York: Columbia University Press.

Houppert, Karen. 2005. *Home Fires Burning: Married to the Military—For Better or for Worse.* New York: Ballantine.

Human Rights Watch. 2004. *The Road to Abu Ghraib.* New York: Human Rights Watch.

Ito, Ruri. 2006. "The Modern Girl Question in 1920s and '30s Okinawa: Colonial Modernity and Women's Mobility." *Journal of Gender Studies* 9: 1–18.

Ito, Ruri, and Yasuyo Morimoto. 2004. "The Modern Girl and Colonial Modernity in East Asia: An International Collaborative Project." *Journal of Gender Studies* 7: 111–114.

Jacobson, Agneta Soderberg. 2005. *Security on Whose Terms: If Men and Women Were Equal.* Stockholm: Kvinna Till Kvinna: Women's Empowerment Projects.

Jargon, Julie. 2003. "The War Within." *Westword*, January 30. http://www .westword.com/issues/2003–01–30/feature.html.

Jehl, Douglas. 2004. "Some Abu Ghraib Abuses Are Traced to Afghanistan." *New York Times*, August 26.

Johnson, Chalmers. 2003. *Sorrows of Empire: Militarism, Secrecy, and the End of the Republic.* New York: Metropol Press.

Joshi, Vijaya. 2005. "Building Opportunities: Women's Organizing, Militarism, and the United Nations Transitional Administration in East Timor." PhD diss., Clark University.

Kang, Stephanie. 2006. "The Swoosh Treads Lightly at Chic Converse." *Globe and Mail* (Toronto), June 23.

Karpinski, Janis. 2005. *One Woman's Army: The Commanding General of Abu Ghraib Tells Her Story.* New York: Hyperion.

Karpinski, Janis. Forthcoming. "Lynndie England in Love." In *Women as Aggressors and Torturers,* ed. Tara McKelvey. Seattle: Seal Press.

Kashiwazaki, Tomoko. 2006. "VAWW Net Japan's Campaign to Bring Justice for the Survivors of Wartime Sexual Slavery." Asia Pacific Forum on Women, Law and Development *Forum News* 19 (January-April): 22.

Kim, Seung-Kyung. 1997. *Class Struggle or Family Struggle: The Lives of Women Factory Workers in South Korea.* London: Cambridge University Press.

Koonz, Claudia. 2003. *The Nazi Conscience.* Cambridge, MA: Harvard University Press.

Koppel, Ted. 2006. "These Guns for Hire." *New York Times,* May 22.

Krauss, Clifford. 2006. "Canada Leader Wins in Extending Afghan Tour." *New York Times,* May 18.

Krosch, Sara L. 2005. "'A New Race of Women': The Challenges of Reintegrating Eritrea's Demobilized Female Combatants." Research paper, Department of International Development, Community and Environment, Clark University.

Kwon, Insook. 1998. "'The New Women's Movement' in 1920s Korea: Rethinking the Relationship Between Imperialism and Women." In "Feminisms and Internationalism," special issue, *Gender and History* 10 (3): 381–405.

———. 2000. "Militarism in My Heart: Militarization of Women's Consciousness and Culture in South Korea." PhD diss., MA, Clark University.

———. 2005. "How Identities and Movement Cultures Became Deeply Saturated with Militarism: Lessons from the Pro-democracy Movement in South Korea." *Asian Journal of Women's Studies* 11 (2): 7–40.

Lang, Amy, and Ceclia Tachi, eds. *What Democracy Looks Like.* New Brunswick, NJ: Rutgers University Press.

Laufer, Peter. 2006. *Mission Rejected: US Soldiers Who Say No to Iraq.* White River Junction, VT: Chelsea Green.

Lawson, Mark. 2006. "The Sex War's New Frontier: We Fight for Equality, Yet Balk at the Death of a Woman in Action in Iraq." *Guardian* (London), May 12.

Lewis, Neil A., and Eric Schmitt. 2004. "Lawyers Decided Bans on Torture Didn't Bind Bush." *New York Times*, June 8.

Lipman, Jana K. Forthcoming. "Guantánamo: A Working Class History of Revolution and Empire, 1939–1979." PhD diss., Yale University.

Lutz, Catherine. 2001. *Homefront: A Military City and the American Twentieth Century*. Boston: Beacon Press.

Lutz, Catherine, ed. Forthcoming. *Undermining Empire: Social Movements against US Overseas Military Installations*. Ithaca: Cornell University Press.

Lutz, Catherine, and Jon Elliston. 2004. "Domestic Terror." In *Interventions: Activists' and Academics' Perspectives on Violence*, ed. Elizabeth Castelli and Janet Jackson. New York: Palgrave Macmillan.

Maley, Jacqueline. 2006. "Sexual Harassment Rife in Armed Forces." *Guardian* (London), May 26.

Manning, Lory. 2005. *Women in the Military: Where They Stand*. 5th ed. Washington, DC: Women's Research and Education Institute.

———. 2006. *Proceedings of the Conference Women in the Military Today*. Washington, DC: Women's Research and Education Institute.

Marshall, Carolyn. 2006. "On a Marine Base, Disbelief over Charges." *New York Times*, May 30.

Mater, Nadire. 2005. *Voices from the Front: Turkish Soldiers on the War with Kurdish Guerrillas*. New York: Palgrave Macmillan.

Mathers, Jennifer G. 2006. "Women, Society, and the Military: Women Soldiers in Post-Soviet Russia." In *Military and Society in Post-Soviet Russia*, ed. Stephen L. Webber and Jennifer G. Mathers, 207–227. Manchester, UK: Manchester University Press.

Mayer, Jane. 2005a. "Outsourcing Torture." *New Yorker*, February 14–21, 106–123.

———. 2005b. "The Memo." *New Yorker*, February 27, 32–41.

———. 2005c. "The Experiment." *New Yorker*, " July 11–18, 60–71.

———. 2006. " The Hidden Power." *New Yorker*, July 3, 44–55.

McKay, Susan, and Dyan Mazurana. 2004. *Where Are the Girls? Girls in Fighting Forces in Northern Uganda, Sierra Leone, and Mozambique*. Montreal: Rights and Democracy.

Miles Foundation. 2004. "Brownback/Fitz Amendment to S. 2400" e-mail message to Miles Foundation mailing list, June 14.

Miles Foundation. http://hometown.aol.com/milesfdn/myhomepage/index.-html.

Moffeit, Miles, and Amy Herder. 2004. "Returning Female GIs Report Rapes, Poor Care." http://www.sirnosir.com/the_film/resistor_84.html.

Moon, Katherine. 1997. *Sex among Allies: Military Prostitution in US-Korea Relations*. New York: Cambridge University Press.

Munn, Jamie. Forthcoming. "The Hegemonic Male and Kosovar Nationalism from 2000–2005." In "Hegemonic Masculinities in International Politics," ed. Juanita Elias, special issue, *Men and Masculinities*.

Murphy, Evelyn, with E. J. Graff. 2005. *Getting Even: Why Women Don't Get Paid Like Men—and What to Do about It*. New York: Simon & Schuster.

New Profile. 2004. *The New Profile Report on Child Recruitment in Israel*. Ramat Ha-Sharon, Israel: New Profile.

No Sweat. www.nosweatapparel.com.

Norton-Taylor, Richard, and Mohammad Alubedy. 2006. "British Alarm as Basra Erupts." *The Guardian Weekly* 174 (4): 1.

Office of the Inspector General, U.S. Department of Defense. 2003. *The Tailhook Report*. New York: St. Martin's.

Ogasawara, Yuko. 1998. *Office Ladies and Salaried Men: Power, Gender, and Work in Japanese Companies*. Berkeley: University of California Press.

Onishi, Norimitsu. 2006. "Japan's Likely Next Premier in Hawkish Stance." *New York Times*, September 2.

Oppel, Richard A. 2006. "Iraqi Accuses U.S. of 'Daily' Attacks against Civilians." *New York Times*, June 2.

Oza, Rupal. 2006. *The Making of Neoliberal India*. New York: Routledge.

Puechguirbal, Nadine. 2003. "Women and War in the Democratic Republic of the Congo." *Signs* 28 (4): 1271–1282.

———. 2006. *Failing to Secure the Peace: Gendered Lessons from Haiti and Iraq*. Boston: Boston Consortium on Gender, Security, and Human Rights.

Refugees International. 2005. *Must Boys Be Boys?* Washington, DC: Refugees International.

Reichberg, Gregory M., Henrik Syse, and Endre Begby. 2006. *The Ethics of War: Classic and Contemporary Readings*. Oxford: Blackwell.

Saar, Eric. 2005. *Inside the Wire: A Military Intelligence Soldier's Eyewitness Account of Life at Guantanamo*. New York: Penguin.

Sands, Philippe. 2005. *Lawless World: America and the Breaking of Global Rules*. London: Penguin.

Sasson-Levy, Orna. 2003. "Feminism and Military Gender Practices: Israeli Women Soldiers in 'Masculine' Roles." *Sociological Inquiry* 73 (3): 440–465.

Schmitt, Eric. 2004. "Abuse Panel Says Rules on Inmates Need Overhaul." *New York Times*, August 25.

Schmitt, Eric, and David S. Cloud. 2006. "Military Inquiry Is Said to Oppose Account of Raid." *New York Times*, May 31.

Sciolino, Elaine. 2006. "Spanish Judge Calls for Closing U.S. Prison at Guantanamo." *New York Times*, June 4.

Seager, Joni. 2003. *The Penguin Atlas of Women in the World*. New York: Penguin.

Shanker, Thom, Eric Schmitt, and Richard A. Oppel. 2006. "Military Expected to Report Marines Killed Iraqi Civilians." *New York Times*. May 26.

Silva, Jennifer Marie. 2006. "Gendered Citizens, Gendered Soldiers? Reproduction, Resistance, and the Cultural Logic of Femininity." Master's thesis, Department of Sociology, University of Virginia.

Singer, P. W. 2003. *Corporate Warriors: The Rise of the Privatized Military Industry*. Ithaca, NY: Cornell University Press.

———. 2006. *Children at War*. Berkeley: University of California Press.

Sjoberg, Laura, and Ann Tickner. Forthcoming. "Feminism." In *International Relations Theories*, ed. Steve Smith, Tim Dunne, and Milja Kurki. London: Oxford University Press.

Solaro, Erin. 2006. *Women in the Line of Fire*. Boston: Seal Press.

Spees, Pam. 2003. "Women's Advocacy in the Creation of the International Criminal Court." *Signs* 28 (4): 1233–1254.

Sperling, Valerie. 2003. "'The Last Refuge of a Scoundrel': Patriotism, Militarism, and the Russian National Idea." *Nations and Nationalism* 9 (April): 235–253.

St. George, Donna. 2006. "Limbs Lost to Enemy Fire, Women Forge New Reality." *Washington Post*, April 18.

Stiehm, Judith Hicks. 2006. *Champions for Peace: Women Winners of the Nobel Peace Prize*. Lanham, MD: Rowman & Littlefield..

Stockford, Marjorie A. 2004. *The Bellwomen: The Story of the Landmark AT&T Sex Discrimination Case*. New Brunswick, NJ: Rutgers University Press.

Stockholm International Peace Research Institute. 2006. *SIPRI Yearbook 2006: Armaments, Disarmament, and International Security*. Oxford: Oxford University Press.

Strasser, Steven, ed. 2004. *The Abu Ghraib Investigations*. New York: Public Affairs.

Taber, Jane. 2006. "Making It Big in the Old Boys' Club." *Globe and Mail* (Toronto), July 7.

Taguba, Antonio. 2004. *Investigation of the 800th Military Police Brigade*. Washington, DC: U.S. Department of Defense.

Taira, Koji. 2003. "The Okinawa Factor in U.S.-Japan Relations," In *The Challenge of Change: East Asia in the New Millennium*, ed. David Arse. Berkeley: Institute of East Asian Studies, University of California, 273–297.

Tickner, J. Ann. 2001. *Gendering World Politics: Issues and Approaches to the Post–Cold War Era*. New York: Columbia University Press.

Turner, Karen Gottschang, with Phan Thanh Hao. 1998. *Even the Women Must Fight: Memories of War from North Vietnam*. New York: Wiley.

Ueno, Chizuko. 2004. *Nationalism and Gender*. Melbourne: Trans Pacific Press.

Wayne, Leslie. 2006. "British Arms Merchant with Passport to the Pentagon." *New York Times*, August 16.

Weapons of Mass Destruction Commission. 2006. *Weapons of Terror: Freeing the World of Nuclear, Biological, and Chemical Arms*. Stockholm: Weapons of Mass Destruction Commission.

Weisman, Robert. 2006. "Colleges Craft Studies to Fit Defense Firms." *Boston Globe*, June 27.

Whitworth, Sandra. 2004. *Men, Militarism and UN Peacekeeping*. Boulder, CO: Lynne Rienner.

Women in Black. 2005. *Women for Peace*. Belgrade: Women in Black.

Women Living Under Muslim Laws. 2006. *Documenting Women's Rights Violations by Non-state Actors: Activist Strategies from Muslim Communities*. Montreal: Rights and Democracy.

Women of Color Resource Center. 2006. *Runway Peace Project: Fashion Resistance to Militarism*. Guide and CD. Oakland, CA: Women of Color Resource Center.

Women Waging Peace and International Alert. 2005. *Inclusive Security: A Toolkit for Advocacy and Action*. Washington, DC: .

Wright, Ann. 2006. "Women Involved in Prisoner Abuse: Perpetrators, Enablers, and Victims." In *Proceedings of the Conference Women in the Military Today, 19–20 May 2005*, ed. Lory Manning, 64–111. Washington, DC: Women's Research and Education Institute.

Wypijewski, JoAnn. 2006. "Judgement Days: Lessons from the Abu Ghraib Courts-Martial." *Harper's*, February, 39–50.

Zahedi, Ahraf. 2006. "State Ideology and the Status of Iranian War Widows." *International Feminist Journal of Politics* 8 (2): 267–286.

INDEX

Aberdeen training base scandal, 106
Abu Ghraib prison, 93; abuses in, 98–
    100; culture of, 105, 108–10; femi-
    nist analysis of, 96–111;
    feminization strategy in, 95–98,
    109, 115; in global network, 95,
    113–15; masculinization in,
    109–10; media coverage of, 99–
    101; officer involvement in,
    93–94; official reports on, 102–4,
    108; public shock at abuses in, 99–
    100; sexuality and, 98–99, 110;
    women soldiers in, 83, 96–97,
    109–10
Addams, Jane, 15
Adidas, 28, 33
Afghanistan: Bagram detention cen-
    ter, 94–95, 97, 113; masculiniza-
    tion in, 52–53; patriarchy in, 134;
    and Resolution 1325, 133–34;
    women soldiers in, 76
African American women: cheap
    labor of, 25; in military, 69
agreements, international, 125–26
Ahn, Christine, 117–18
AIDS. *See* HIV/AIDS
Air Force Academy, U.S., 107, 108
Algeria, 8
American Historical Association, 43
American Political Science Associa-
    tion, 44

Amnesty International, 128
Anbar, Iraq, 112
antiglobalization, 3
Argentina, 113, 122, 123
arms sales, 157–58
Article 9, of Japanese constitution,
    138–40, 146
Asahi Shimbun, 57
Asian Journal of Women's Studies, 141
Asian women, 141
Asia Pacific Forum on Women, Law
    and Development, 142
Association for Asian Studies, 44
AT&T, 7
Australia, 8

baby socks, militarization of, 143–44
"bad apple" explanation, 101–2
BAE Systems, 6–7
Bagram detention center, Afghani-
    stan, 94–95, 97, 113
Bailes, Alyson, 158–59
Balch, Emily Greene, 15
Ballinger, Jeff, 35–37
Bata, 36–37
Beijing Conference on Women
    (1995), 140
Beijing Plus Five conference (2000),
    140
Belgrade Women in Black, 127

ABOUT THE AUTHOR

Cynthia Enloe is Research Professor of International Development at Clark University in Massachusetts, where she has chaired both the Department of Government and the Women's Studies Program. She is the author of ten books, including *Bananas, Beaches, and Bases, Maneuvers: The International Politics of Militarizing Women's Lives,* and *The Curious Feminist: Searching for Women in a New Age of Empire.* Her books and articles have been translated into Japanese, Turkish, Korean, German, and Spanish.